THE REMARKABLE KENNEDYS
by JOE McCARTHY

Here is the complete life story of John Kennedy. Senator Kennedy, young, Catholic and heir to a multi-million dollar fortune, is perhaps the most controversial man in politics today. In **The Remarkable Kennedys,** top reporter Joe McCarthy gives a fair-minded appraisal of the young senator from Massachusetts—his life and views—and tells all about the people closest to him: his lovely wife, Jackie; his relentless, crusading brother, Bob, investigator for the Senate Rackets Committee; his sister Pat, who married Hollywood actor Peter Lawford; and his ambassador father, Joe, who acquired a fortune of 250 million dollars, married the mayor of Boston's daughter, and became a close advisor to Franklin Roosevelt.

But most of all, this is the story of John Kennedy—his early life in a close-knit, ambitious family; his initiation into a political career he never wanted; and his rapid—some say too rapid—rise to national fame. **The Remarkable Kennedys** is an indispensable book for anyone interested in the future of American politics.

JOE McCARTHY, a former war correspondent, is a top reporter and writer of non-fiction. Since 1948 he has contributed more than 100 articles to **Look, Life, Reader's Digest, Holiday, McCall's** and other national magazines. He lives with his wife and four children in Blue Point, Long Island.

THE REMARKABLE
KENNEDYS

JOE McCARTHY

POPULAR LIBRARY • NEW YORK

POPULAR LIBRARY EDITION
Published in August, 1960

© 1960 by Joe McCarthy

Library of Congress Catalog Card Number: 60-8394

Published by arrangement with The Dial Press, Inc.

The Dial Press edition published in February, 1960

First printing: February, 1960

The material by William V. Shannon is reprinted from the New York POST and used with the permission of the author.

The excerpt from "Democratic Forecast: A Catholic in 1960" by Fletcher Knebel is reprinted from LOOK, March 3, 1959 and used with the permission of the publishers.

The editorial from the New York HERALD TRIBUNE is reprinted from the issue of January 10, 1960, with the permission of the publishers.

Cover photo: Wide World

CONTENTS

THE REMARKABLE KENNEDYS

1

A TALK WITH THE AMBASSADOR

DURING an election campaign in his Massachusetts constituency, Senator John Fitzgerald Kennedy was driving through South Boston with John E. Powers, the local Democratic leader. Powers pointed out the house where he was born. "Johnny, you're always boasting about your humble origin," the Senator said, "but that's a much nicer house than the one I was born in on Beals Street in Brookline. I came up the hard way."

"Yeah," Powers said. "You came up the hard way. One morning they didn't bring you your breakfast in bed."

Kennedy was born in the Beals Street house in Brookline, a fashionable but not especially swanky suburb of Boston, on May 29, 1917, which will make him forty-three at the time of the 1960 Democratic convention. (Theodore Roosevelt, our youngest President, was in the White House at forty-two, but Roosevelt was not elected to the highest office at that age; he moved up from the vice-presidency when William McKinley was assassinated, much to the surprise of the party bosses who thought they had safely stowed away Teddy and his liberal reform ideas in the obscurity of the Number Two spot.) Last year Senator Kennedy and his pretty wife, Jacqueline, whom everybody calls Jackie, and their two-year-old daughter, Caroline, came up from Washington to spend his forty-second birthday at Hyannis Port on Cape Cod where he and his younger brother, Robert, the family's other fast-rising public figure, have houses next to the rambling beachfront home of their father, Joseph P. Kennedy. While their nine children were growing up, Rose and Joe Kennedy lived in many places and they now list their winter house at Palm Beach as their official residence, but they have always looked upon Hyannis Port, where they have spent their summers since the 1920s, as their real home.

Jack Kennedy's birthday was a bright and warm day. In the morning he sat alone in the sun on the porch of his father's house, reading *The Charterhouse of Parma*. At noon, he put aside his book to greet a reporter for a national magazine who was preparing a series of articles on the Kennedys. The reporter mentioned an exclusive inside story in the previous week's *Time* and *Life* about Sam Rayburn and Harry Truman agreeing during a ride downtown in a limousine after a Washington dinner party that the Democratic presidential candidate should be either Stuart Symington or Lyndon Johnson. Kennedy grinned.

"I heard Lyndon wasn't too happy about that story," he said. "Lyndon isn't sure people will like the idea of two old timers like Rayburn and Truman deciding, in the back seat of a Cadillac, who will be the next President of the United States."

Kennedy did not need to add that he has steered his own political course carefully away from close associations with older party leaders like Rayburn and Truman for just that reason; he feels that being identified as a protégé of the bosses does a young politician no good with the modern voting public. Such a lonely and roundabout road is a difficult one for an ambitious office seeker to climb, and; as the stake gets bigger and the need for compromises and bargaining within the party becomes more urgent, Kennedy is finding his chosen path harder to stick to. But thus far, in Massachusetts at least, his avoidance of machine politics and his unpoliticianlike Ivy League appearance and casual platform manner have given him a powerful appeal as a vote getter. During the Eisenhower landslide of 1952, the thirty-five-year-old Kennedy was the only Democratic winner in his state, astounding the experts by beating Ike's own right hand man, Henry Cabot Lodge, for the Senate. In 1958, Jack was re-elected by 870,000 votes, the largest plurality of any candidate from either party in the history of Massachusetts.

"How did he do it?" Thomas Winship wrote in the *Boston Globe* the following Sunday. "It seemed that perhaps the biggest ingredient was Kennedy's ability to present the public image of being both a safe middle-of-the-roader, standing high above party (not unlike the early Eisenhower image) and a red hot liberal. Even before returns came in, there was interesting proof of Kennedy's being able to sell himself as a Democrat in a buttoned-down collar shirt for whom a Republican could vote without permanently tainting himself and, at the same time, to hold city Democrats and Cambridge liberals. A week before the election he was the only state office-holder to match the endorsement standards of the Massachusetts Americans for Democratic Action. After winning A.D.A. support, he landed an editorial in the staunch Republican *Boston Herald*, a paper that often editorializes against the dangers of the A.D.A. on the American scene."

While Jack and the magazine reporter were talking, Jackie Kennedy and Caroline, and Caroline's nursemaid, appeared in the driveway in front of the porch. The Senator's father and mother came out of the house to see their grandchild. Rose Kennedy, a quiet woman, is youthful for her years. When her nine children were young, she was introduced in Washington to John Boettiger, then Franklin D. Roosevelt's son-in-law, who glanced at her trim figure and said, "Now I believe in the stork." The Ambassador, as her husband is called by people around the Kennedys to distinguish him from the Senator, is now seventy-one years old. A vigorous and colorful man, he rides horseback or plays eighteen holes of golf every day and travels widely, supervising by long distance telephone the affairs of the New York office that manages his and his children's vast financial and real estate holdings. He was planning to leave Hyannis Port shortly after Jack's birthday to divide the summer between a trip to Lake Tahoe and a stay at the home he maintains on the French Riviera. Discussing his tax problem with an acquaintance recently, Joe Kennedy complained that taxes are eating up so much of his income that he had to dip into his capital to pay his living expenses. "And," he added, jabbing his finger into the other man's shoulder, "there are God-damned few people in this whole world that have a bigger income than I've got." In 1957, in a survey of American multimillionaires, *Fortune* magazine bracketed him with Irenee and William du Pont, Howard Hughes and the late Sid Richardson, estimating his wealth at around 250 millions. This is one of the very few large fortunes in the world that do not stem mainly from oil or from inheritance. Kennedy made his first millions with Wall Street trading and private banking in the boom of the Twenties and later expanded his wealth in various business ventures, moving picture production, theaters, imported liquors and real estate. When his children reached the age of twenty-one, each of them received a million dollar trust fund with no strings attached. "I put them in a position where each one of them could spit in my eye and tell me where to go, and there was nothing to prevent them from becoming rich, idle bums if they wanted to," he has said. "Luckily, they didn't turn out that way."

If few people in the world, as he says, have a bigger income than Kennedy, it is also probable that few successful financiers have been able to combine their money-making with the accumulation of such a wealth of rich experience in the broader realms of national and world affairs as he has gathered over the years. Joe Kennedy was in the thick of the New Deal as Roosevelt's close advisor and constant dinner companion, as organizer and first chairman of the Securities Exchange Commission; and, as head of the Maritime Commission, he settled $73,000,000 in shipping claims against the government for $750,000 and threw a punch at Harry Bridges during a hotel room labor argument. Then he was Ambassador to the Court of St. James during the outbreak of World War II. Before F.D.R. decided to run for a third term, Kennedy was widely mentioned as a possible Democratic candidate for the presidency in the 1940 election.

Now, with so much behind him, he was standing in the sun at Hyannis Port talking with a son who had been named in that month's Gallup poll as the leading Democratic candidate for president in 1960. The next Kennedy son, Robert, had gained so much prominence as the relentless inquisitor of the Senate Rackets Committee that a West Coast lawyer wrote to Jack advising the Senator to step aside and let his younger brother run for the presidency. Jack wrote back to him, "I am taking your recommendation under advisement. I have consulted Bobby about it, and, to my dismay, the idea appeals to him." One of Joe Kennedy's sons-in-law, Robert Sargent Shriver, Jr., of Chicago, husband of his daughter, Eunice, was being talked about as the next governor of Illinois. Another daughter, Patricia, was married to a Hollywood movie and television star, Peter Lawford, and living in the palatial beach home at Santa Monica that was built for the late film tycoon, Louis B. Mayer.

The quiet oldest girl, and the only unmarried one, Rosemary, was teaching in a school for retarded children in Wisconsin. The youngest daughter, Jean, married to a scion of a wealthy New York barge and tug boat family, Steve Smith, was living in Washington where her husband works on Jack's campaign staff. The youngest Kennedy, Edward Moore, better known as Teddy and named after the late Eddie Moore, his father's devoted aide-de-camp over the years in Wall Street, Washington and London, was at that time finishing law studies at the University of Virginia. In partnership with his friend, Varick Tunney, son of Gene, the former heavyweight champion, Teddy had just won the law school's annual mock trial competition. "Teddy will do well in anything he chooses," Bobby says. Teddy is choosing politics.

Two outstanding Kennedy children are dead. The oldest one in the family was Joseph P. Kennedy, Jr., a big, burly and handsome fellow whose charm is remembered by everyone who knew him. He was planning a political career when he became a Navy flyer in World War II. He volunteered for a dangerous experimental mission against a German V-2 rocket base. During the flight, his plane exploded in mid-air. His body was never recovered. After young Joe's death, Secretary of the Navy James V. Forrestal wrote to his father, "Your boy was unusual in every respect. He had guts and character and an extraordinary personality."

The second Kennedy daughter, two years younger than Rosemary and three years younger than Jack, was Kathleen. A Frenchman who knew the Ambassador's daughters when they were in London said of them, "Eunice is the most intellectual and Pat's the prettiest, but Kathleen is the one you remember." In London, Kathleen met the Marquess of Hartington, son and heir of the Duke of Devonshire, a high ranking peer who was then regarded in court circles as a suitable suitor for Crown Princess Elizabeth. During the war, when Kathleen came back to Britain as a Red Cross worker, she and the Marquess were married. A few months later, he was killed in infantry action in Normandy where he was an officer in the Coldstream Guards. In 1948, Kathleen died in a plane crash in France.

If Kathleen and her husband had lived, in her high position in British aristocracy as the Duchess of Devonshire she would be today first lady in waiting to Queen Elizabeth and Mistress of the Royal Robes. It is likely that in succeeding to his father's title, the Marquess would have also been elected to the late Duke's office as grand master of the craft of Freemasons. Joe Kennedy was asked recently how it would feel to be the father of the first Catholic president of the United States. "That's nothing," he said. "If Kathleen and her husband were living, I'd also be the father of the Duchess of Devonshire and the father-in-law of the head of all the Masons in the world."

In short, a family saga-type work of fiction on a clan like the Kennedys—a self-made multimillionaire father with a beautiful wife and nine children and international fame as a diplomat, daughters who married a nobleman, a Hollywood star, and a prospective governor of Illinois, a son who makes headlines as a spectacular investigator of labor racketeers, and, to top it all, another son who becomes a glamorous young candidate for President of the United States—such a novel would be dismissed by editors and reviewers as far-fetched. The Kennedy story is also over-lavishly embellished with a variety of richly dramatic scenes that even Edna Ferber, with all the stops pulled out, would not dare to pack within the covers of her most sweeping epic: the Ambassador, at the height of his career, hastily resigning from his post in London and being forced out of public life because he was the only top figure in Roosevelt's government who dared to speak out against our involvement in the European war; Jack's incredible and harrowing survival in the South Pacific where he was lost for six days and given up for dead after his PT boat was wrecked in enemy waters by a Japanese destroyer; Young Joe turning down a chance to go home after two tours of air combat duty to volunteer eagerly for his last dangerous mission; Bobby quitting officer training school and enlisting as a lowly seaman so that he could serve on the new destroyer named after his heroic dead brother; the emotional scenes in both families when the devoutly Catholic Kennedys' Kathleen decided to marry the son of the relentlessly Protestant Duke of Devonshire; Old Joe, bowed with grief, rushing from Paris to the village of Privas in Southern France to identify Kathleen's body when it was carried down from the scene of the mountainside plane crash in a peasant's farm cart; Jack giving up his plans to be a writer and going into politics because he felt an obligation to carry on in the place of Young Joe, who had always wanted to be President of the United States; Patricia on a round-the-world tour with a girl companion abruptly turning back from the trip in Tokyo and hurrying home to accept Peter Lawford's marriage proposal; Rose Fitzgerald Kennedy campaigning on street corners for her son in his battle for the Senate against Henry Cabot Lodge, whose grandfather had narrowly beaten Jack's grandfather, John F. Fitzgerald, in a fight for the same Senate seat back in 1916; the uproar at the 1956 Democratic convention in Chicago when Jack came from nowhere to within 38½ votes from the vice-presidential nomination on the second ballot; Jack on his sick bed, after a serious spinal operation that almost took his life, doggedly writing the Pulitzer Prize-winning book, *Profiles In Courage*, and Jack, in white tie, speaking in the Waldorf Astoria from the same platform with Nelson Rockefeller and quoting Al Smith on religious bigotry, "The Catholics of the country can stand it. The Jews can stand it. But the United States of America cannot stand it."

Jack introduced the reporter who was visiting him at Hyannis Port to his wife and to his parents. Joe was taking Jack and Jackie out on his cabin cruiser for a swim and a clam chowder lunch and he invited the reporter to join them. The Senator and his wife went ahead to the boat dock with Caroline and her nursemaid and Joe and the reporter talked together as they followed them.

"I know the first question you're going to ask me," Joe said, "and I'll tell you right now I don't know the answer to it, if there is one. You're going to ask me if we had some special formula or plan for bringing up our children. Of course I'm proud of our kids and what they're doing—certainly it's a lot better than selling ham and eggs. But I don't know if we did anything in raising them that other parents don't do. My wife is a deeply religious woman and she may have given more time and care to their spiritual training than some mothers do. And both of us tried to be interested in what they were doing. If one of them was in a school play or playing in a crucial school football game, we made it a point to be there."

"You have an unusually close family," the reporter said.

"They've always been very close to each other," Kennedy said. "The girls are scattered all over the country now but they still talk to each other on the phone twice a week. Jack and Bobby and Teddy are always together. All of them have always seemed to have a lot of fun and enjoyment out of being with each other, more so than you find in most big families. You hear a lot today about togetherness. Long before it became a slogan, I guess we had it. Another thing: we gave them responsibility when they were young. Joe and Jack were out in sail boats alone here at Hyannis Port when they were so small you couldn't see their heads. It looked from the shore as if the boats were empty. You remember the *Athenia*, the British ship that was sunk by the Germans right after war was declared in 1939? Jack was with me in London at the time. He was only twenty-one, still in Harvard, but I sent him up to Glasgow to handle the whole job of taking care of the American survivors and finding out from them what had happened. And he handled it well, too. One of the things I did with the children to give them a sense of responsibility was to offer each one of them a thousand dollars for not smoking and another thousand for not drinking until they reached the age of twenty-one. I never checked up on them or asked them about it. It was done on the honor system. On each one's twenty-first birthday, I wrote out two checks and handed them to the child and it was up to them to decide whether they could keep the checks. Two of the kids handed the checks back to me. Well, here's the boat. We'll take a run over to Wianno or Craigville, where the water's a little warmer at this time of year, and we can anchor there and have a swim before lunch. I brought a pair of trunks that ought to fit you."

The Ambassador greeted the man who acts as the skipper of the cruiser and complimented him on its ship-shape appearance. "We haven't used this boat in five years," he said to the reporter. "I had it put in the water this summer so the grandchildren could have the use of it." After waving good-bye to Caroline, Jackie and Jack went up to the front of the boat to stretch out in the sun. Joe and the reporter sat down in the stern and resumed their conversation. The reporter asked how Jack had happened to go into politics. Joe looked at him in surprise.

"I thought everybody knows about that," Kennedy said. "Jack went into politics because Young Joe died. Young Joe was going to be the politician in the family. When he died, Jack took his place."

"That was what I had heard," the reporter said. "I was just wondering if you might have had a different idea about it."

"Have you seen that book about Joe that Jack put together after his death, the book called *As We Remember Joe?* I've never been able to read that book. I tried to look at it again the other night when I heard you were coming up here, because I knew you'd be asking me about Joe, but I had to put it down after the first couple of pages. It's too much for me. I never got over that boy's death. Joe used to talk about being president some day, and a lot of smart people thought he would make it. He was altogether different from Jack, more dynamic, more sociable and easy going. Jack in those days back there when he was getting out of college was rather shy, withdrawn and quiet. His mother and I couldn't picture him as a politician. We were sure he'd be a teacher or a writer. I'll never forget the day when Jack started his first campaign in the congressional primary in Boston. I was in Maverick Square in East Boston, talking with a man I knew in front of the bank we had there, and I look across the street and see Jack, getting out of a car and walking up to a bunch of hard boiled guys who are standing on the corner and putting his hand out and introducing himself and asking for their vote. I remember saying to the man who was with me that I would have given odds of five thousand to one that this thing we were seeing could never have happened. I never thought Jack had it in him."

The reporter mentioned a conversation he had in Washington a few days previously with Justice William O. Douglas of the Supreme Court, a close friend of the Kennedys who was first brought to Washington by Joe to work with the SEC. Justice Douglas had commented on the fact that all of Kennedy's sons had been interested in government careers rather than in business where their father had made his fortune. He suggested that the young Kennedys might have been pointed toward Washington rather than toward Wall Street because in his own career Joe had found more satisfaction in his government work than in business and finance.

"I don't know about that," Joe said. "I certainly have encouraged the boys' interest in public service because I honestly feel—and this is no baloney—that we owe a great debt to our government. But I don't think I really pushed my sons in any particular direction. I'd be very happy if Teddy wanted to get into my business instead of politics. I need somebody in the family to take over my business. It's a big thing and it would be nice if one of my own flesh and blood was running it. But you've got to remember that politics comes natural to these boys. They grew up with it and so did I. Both of their grandfathers were politicians and they heard a lot of politics from me when I was working for Roosevelt. God knows there was a lot to talk about in those days. Do you remember the stink that was raised by labor people when I was chairman of the Maritime Commission and I ordered a bunch of seamen on an American ship in

South America put into irons because they pulled a strike on the captain? I did it because the strike had nothing to do with the ship or the way it was being run. They were striking in sympathy with a South American longshoremen's fight that had nothing to do with us. I asked Roosevelt what he would do if I was in the wrong. He said, 'I won't do anything. If you're wrong, you'll have to swing for it.' And he was absolutely right, of course. There's no reason why the presidency should be forced to take the rap for a decision that was made downstairs. I didn't care too much for some of the people around him, but Roosevelt was a good man."

The cruiser was nearing Craigville Beach and the skipper turned off the motor and dropped anchor. The ocean at Cape Cod is cold in May but Joe was the first one to dive into the water and the last one to climb back onto the boat. Then he mixed gin rickeys for everybody but Jack, who seldom drinks anything alcoholic and never smokes. During the luncheon that followed, the father and son exchanged Washington gossip and presidential campaign speculation. Jackie listened to them with interest but had little to say. At one point, when Jack mentioned that he was to speak at a hat makers' union convention the following week, she said to him, "You'd better remember to buy yourself a hat before you go there."

The Ambassador mentioned to the Senator a discussion he had had recently with Herbert Hoover about the Catholic issue, or, as the late Paul Dever, former governor and Democratic leader of Massachusetts, used to call it, "the canonical impediment." Hoover said, according to Joe, that he believes that Catholicism today is not as much of a handicap to a presidential candidate as most people think. He had quoted figures to Kennedy which showed that Al Smith in 1928 had won a much larger popular vote than politicians today give him credit for getting. The reporter passed on to the Kennedys a rather novel theory about the political weight of Jack's Catholicism that he had heard from Arthur M. Schlesinger, Jr., the Harvard political historian and Democratic party adviser. Schlesinger feels that the Senator's religious denomination has been a help rather than a hindrance to his career.

"Jack's Catholicism is the very thing that has brought him into prominence," Schlesinger says. "Looking as Jack does and talking as he does, a liberal-minded senator from New

England who went to Choate School and Harvard and comes from a wealthy family—if he were just another Protestant, nobody would pay much attention to him. But being a Catholic, Jack is a controversial figure. That's why everybody is interested in him."

Jack chewed thoughtfully on the frame of his sun glasses and nodded.

"That's right, up to now," he said. "But from now on I wouldn't be so sure about it."

The reporter turned to Joe Kennedy and said, "I've seen you quoted as saying that the reason you moved your family out of Boston in the Twenties was the anti-Catholic and anti-Irish prejudice in Massachusetts."

"That's exactly why I left Boston," Joe said. "I felt it was no place to bring up Irish Catholic children. I didn't want them to go through what I had to go through when I was growing up there. They tell me it's better now, but at that time the social and economic discrimination was shocking. I know so many Irish guys in Boston with real talent and ability that never got to first base only because of their race and religion. In New York or Chicago, they would have been big men. But, as I say, things must be changing in Boston. A few years ago Jack was elected to the Board of Overseers at Harvard, which would have been unheard of in my day. It seems to me that if a Catholic can be elected to the Board of Overseers at Harvard, he can be elected to anything. Didn't you go to a meeting of the Overseers a couple of weeks ago, Jack?"

"I was there," Jack said. "It was very interesting. I delivered a lengthy report on what's going on in the astronomy department. I saw Professor Holcombe and he asked to be remembered to you, Dad."

"Professor Holcombe had his troubles with me when I was in Harvard," the Ambassador said. "You know, he taught me and he taught all four of our boys and I was probably the worst student of the whole lot. I did so poorly at Harvard in a course in banking and finance, the very thing I made my living in later, that I had to drop out of it after one semester. Jack was a good student, but he didn't get it from me. He was reading Billy Whiskers books before he even went to school. I remember when he was a little bit of a shaver trying to find out where the Canary Islands were because he had read something about them in a Billy Whiskers book. Me, I had never heard of the Canary Islands at the time."

"I was talking with Professor Holcombe myself not long ago," the reporter said, "Professor Holcombe and a few other professors in the Faculty Club at Cambridge, and we were talking about Jack. I asked them, if, in their opinion, Jack was qualified, intellectually, spiritually, and emotionally, to serve as President of the United States. They all agreed that they felt he was as well equipped, and maybe better equipped for the job, as any President in many years has been before he was elected. They pointed out that most of our great Presidents grew in stature after they were in the White House. They said they couldn't think of any one who was better than Kennedy at the time he went into office."

"What are the qualifications for the presidency?" the Ambassador said.

"I was talking about that with a Senator in Washington," the reporter said. "You know what he said? He said, 'After all, the work of the president itself is not too demanding. The government more or less runs itself. What we need more than anything else in the White House is a man who has the power to rally the people in the time of a crisis, a man who can inspire them and encourage them and hold them together.' "

"Bosh!" Joe Kennedy said.

"You're kidding!" Jack said. "Was he serious? In other words, all we need is a reassuring speechmaker."

"I've seen the president's job from the inside and I think I know what it requires," Joe Kennedy said. "In the presidency, you need a man with both the wide factual knowledge and the courage to make the right decisions and to make them stick. The biggest part of the president's job is stepping into fights between the Secretary of State and the Secretary of Defense, between the Secretary of the Treasury and the Federal Reserve System, or between the Secretary of the Army and the Secretary of Navy, and putting his fist down and deciding what is going to be done—calmly and objectively, basing his decision on his own careful study of the issues without taking anybody's word for it and without being influenced by personal feelings. Jack has that in him. That's why I'm for him. If he didn't have that in him, if he was just a nice fellow with a nice appearance and a nice way of getting along with people, I wouldn't be bothered with him, even though he is my own son."

The boat turned back toward Hyannis Port and the talk turned toward other things. "Jack hasn't had it as easy as a lot of people think," the Ambassador said. "He ran against Lodge for the Senate because nobody else wanted the nomination. Lodge was supposed to be unbeatable in Massachusetts and Paul Dever, who was the big Democrat at the time and the logical candidate for the Senate, wanted no part of him. That spring when Lodge heard that Jack was thinking of running against him, he sent word to me through a friend of mine that I'd only be wasting my money backing Jack. He said nobody had a chance against him and a lot of the Irish in Boston felt the same way. All I ever heard when I was growing up in Boston was how Lodge's grandfather had helped to put the stained glass windows into the Gate of Heaven Church in South Boston and they were still talking about those same stained glass windows in 1952. So if you think it was easy for Jack to run against Lodge, you've got another think coming."

It was recalled that the Boston Irish had even deserted their popular champion, James Michael Curley, to support Lodge in his first race for the Senate in 1936, a campaign in which the confident Curley had referred to the young Lodge as "Little Boy Blue." That was also the campaign in which Curley skillfully talked his way out of a serious crisis when he was accused by an opponent before an aroused Irish audience in South Boston of preferring the music of "The Isle of Capri" to "The Wearing of the Green". The band preceding Curley's car in that year's St. Patrick's Day parade had played "The Isle of Capri" because it didn't know his customary theme song, "Tammany," and South Boston had blamed him for the choice of the un-Irish tune. Taking over the platform, Curley chided the audience for not knowing that "The Isle of Capri" had been composed by "a famous Irish musician." He was so convincing that the meeting ended with Curley leading the whole gathering as it loudly sang "The Isle of Capri." He admitted privately later that he had no idea of who had written the song.

"There'll never be anybody again like Curley," Jack Kennedy said. "You remember that story about what he said when he heard that Governor Cox had appointed as district attorney of Middlesex County Leverett Saltonstall's uncle,

Endicott Peabody Saltonstall? Curley said, 'All three of them?' "

"Getting back to Lodge," the reporter said to the Ambassador, "it's been said and written many times that you gave a big donation to Senator Joe McCarthy in 1952 to keep him from campaigning for the Republicans against Jack in Massachusetts that year."

"Baloney," the Ambassador said. "I gave Joe McCarthy a small contribution, sure, but it was only a couple of thousand dollars and I didn't give it to him to keep him out of Massachusetts. I gave it to him because a mutual friend of ours, Westbrook Pegler, asked me to give it to him and because I liked the fight he was putting up against Communists in our government. Nobody had to pay McCarthy to keep him from working for Lodge. There was no love between them. I remember that McCarthy told my son Bobby that year that if the Republican National Committee asked him to speak for them in Massachusetts he would have to do it. They didn't ask him to do it because Lodge didn't want him. If you want my opinion, Lodge made a big mistake. McCarthy would have gotten him a lot of votes."

The boat eased up to the dock and Jack and Jackie began to collect the lunch baskets, towels and bathing suits.

"I don't suppose I've told you anything you didn't already know," the Ambassador said to the reporter. "Have you talked to any of Jack's friends?"

"Yes, and to some of his enemies, too," the reporter said.

"Jack's enemies wouldn't have much to tell you," the Ambassador said. "Now if you talked to my enemies, that would be something else again. They could tell you plenty."

2

GO, GO, GO

IF Joe Kennedy feels that he has given his children nothing particularly worth mentioning that other parents don't give to their children, he overlooks one big item. Everybody who knows the Kennedys talks about the fierceness of the deep competitive drive that the father has instilled in the sons. As youngsters, two of them were sent away from the dinner table at Hyannis Port in disgrace one evening because they had not made an all-out effort to win a sailing race that afternoon. A few years ago Bob Kennedy worked exceptionally hard for a period of more than three months without a day off from his job as counsel of the Senate rackets committee, or, as Jimmy Hoffa used to call it, McClellan's Playhouse 90. Exhausted, he went to Hyannis Port for a weekend. By Sunday afternoon, he was feeling better, but he decided to take one more day of rest. On Monday morning, when the Ambassador came in from his daily horseback ride and found Bob sitting in the living room, he glared at his son and said to him, "What's the big idea of sitting around up here on the Cape when you should be at your job in Washington?"

"Whether it's a subcommittee hearing or a game of touch football at the Washington Monument, they're out for blood," a close friend of the family says. A Washington reporter sums up the Kennedys with a line from a pep talk that he overheard Bob giving to one of his seven small children. "Let's swing higher and try for a new record," Bob said. "A Kennedy shouldn't be scared." The many stories of their teeth-gritting physical tenacity are almost unbelievable. Kenny O'Donnell, Bob's assistant on the McClellan committee and his room mate and football team mate at Harvard, recalls one day in a practice scrimmage at Soldiers' Field when Bob tried to block an opposing back near the sidelines and crashed into an equipment wagon. He picked himself up and returned to his position at end. Three plays later, he collapsed and was carried from the field. An examination showed that he had been playing with a broken leg. Jack damaged his health at Harvard by sneaking out of the college infirmary, where he was confined with grippe and a high fever, to practice nightly so that he could compete for a place on the swimming team in the meet with Yale. "He was on a light diet at the infirmary because of his fever and this worried him," his friend, Torbert Macdonald, recalls. "He was afraid he wouldn't be strong enough to win the swimming trials. So he made me smuggle malted milks and steaks into the infirmary. Then he'd get me to help him disappear from his room for an hour. He would rush to the Indoor Athletic Building, swim several laps in the pool, and rush back to the infirmary so that he would be back in bed before the nurse came around to take his temperature and give him his medicine." Unfortunately, Jack did not get into the Yale meet. He was beaten in the competition by Richard Tregaskis, who later became a famed war correspondent and author of the best-selling *Guadalcanal Diary*. Kennedy was ill for the rest of the college year.

Several magazine articles and a Navy Log television show have described the ordeal Jack went through in 1943 when he and the other survivors of his wrecked PT boat were lost for six days in the Japanese-held area of the Solomon Islands. None of these accounts mentioned Kennedy's behavior after he was rescued, which seemed to Navy men at the time more incredible than his survival. As was customary in such cases, he and his crew were ordered back to the States. Jack refused to go. Crippled by an old football spinal injury that had been dislocated again in the torpedo boat crash, he insisted upon staying on in the South Pacific, taking charge of a new PT and another crew and spending several more months in combat. Some fellow officers wondered if the back injury had also affected his mind. Similarly, the oldest Kennedy boy, Young Joe, turned down orders to return to stateside duty after two full tours of Naval air combat in Europe in order to volunteer for the experimental mission in which he was killed. Young Joe's luggage had been placed on a New York-bound transport ship when he asked for the job of piloting an explosive-laden Liberator PBY4 that was to be aimed at a German V-2 rocket base, and guided into a crash dive on the target by radio control after its flyers parachuted from it.

Bob Kennedy's strong drive and determination to win shows up clearly in an investigative hearing or in the heat of a campaign. ("Bobby's as hard as nails," his father says.) Jack's keyed-up, almost compulsive, competitiveness is usually concealed by his affable and deceptively casual manner. Few Washington figures work as intensively at their politics as he does; in the past four years, he has taken only one vacation that lasted for two consecutive weeks. One day before his spinal injury's pain was eased by operations and a series of novocaine injections, Jack made his way on crutches to Cleveland to speak at a luncheon, hurried back to Washington in the afternoon to vote on a bill in the Senate and flew to Cleveland again in the evening to appear at a political dinner. Even during the long months of recuperation after his operations in 1955, when he was forced to remain on his back in bed, the Senator was unable to refrain from work. That was when he wrote his Pulitzer prizewinning historical book, *Profiles in Courage*.

"Jack's success in politics ever since his first campaign for Congress in 1946 has been entirely due to hard work and long hours," one of his associates says. "I don't think any other politician at any time ever shook so many hands in so many small villages and towns or ever shaved in the men's rooms of so many filling stations and bowling alleys."

John T. Galvin, a Boston public relations counsel who has been a Kennedy volunteer worker since the Senator made his political debut, was recalling recently a bright and pleasant autumn Saturday afternoon when the Harvard-Princeton football game was being played at Princeton. Galvin found Kennedy alone in Boston. "I knew how much Jack wanted to be at that football game," Galvin said. "This was before he was married, and there were any number of gorgeous girls who would have dropped everything to go to Princeton with him that day and he knew it. I asked him what the hell he was doing hanging around in Boston on a beautiful Saturday like that when he could have been living it up at the game with a nice number hanging onto his arm, and driving into New York afterwards for dinner at Twenty One or the Stork Club. You know what he said? He said he had to make a speech to a group of plumbers in the South End that night."

Another Boston friend and admirer who has traveled through Massachusetts with the Senator on his extensive election campaigns says, "You're driving with Jack doing eighty miles an hour, and he keeps asking you to go faster because he's already ten minutes late at the next town. A motorcycle cop starts chasing you, so you stop and get out, and, miraculously, you fast-talk the cop into letting you go on. Naturally, you're feeling rather proud of yourself for accomplishing such a feat. A few miles further on, you come to a railroad crossing where the red light is flashing and the bell is ringing. Jack says, 'Come on, we've got to beat that train.' So you step on it and race to the crossing, but the locomotive gets there a couple of inches ahead of you and you just miss hitting it. Jack grits his teeth in disgust. 'If you hadn't wasted so much time back there talking to that cop, we would have made it,' he says."

Where does the Kennedy competitive drive come from? Most probably it stems originally from the chafing, frustrating atmosphere of anti-Irish and anti-Catholic prejudice in Boston fifty years ago that made the young Joe Kennedy determined to push himself and his children to a place at the top of the world where they would not have to take a back seat for anybody. A vivid, if bitter, comment on Boston was made recently by a woman who comes from there. Listening at a Long Island cocktail party to an admiring description of the cobblestone pavement on Yankee Protestant Beacon Hill, she remarked quietly, "Those aren't cobblestones. Those are Irish heads."

The air in Boston is somewhat clearer now; some Irish Catholics at Harvard are now permitted to row on the varsity crew and since World War II some of them have been elected to membership in the better clubs, such as The Fly and The Gas House. In the Twenties and Thirties, the only Irishmen seen around those sanctuaries were the boys who delivered the ice and the White Rock. But it is still said that Boston Irish, who comprise seventy-five percent of the city's population, are the largest minority group anywhere. The well-known jingle about Boston being the place where the Lowells speak only to the Cabots and the Cabots only to God was first delivered by a Massachusetts Irish Catholic at a Holy Cross College alumni banquet. When Joe Kennedy was young, help wanted advertisements in the Boston newspapers frequently carried the line, "Protestants only" or "No Irish need apply." The same newspapers carefully divided the Sunday social news into two sections, one of the Proper Bostonians and another for the Irish.

Resentment probably burned hotter in Joe Kennedy than in most of the Boston Irish of his generation because he associated more closely with the Yankee Brahmins than did most Irish of his time. Consequently, he was more exposed to slurs, more aware from first-hand experience of the cool condescension with which Beacon Hill looked down on people of his religion and racial background. It was unusual in 1908 for Boston Irish boys to go to Harvard, as Kennèdy did. If they were able to go to college at all, they invariably went to the Jesuits at Boston College. The few that did go to Harvard commuted to their classes in Cambridge by street car from their homes in Dorchester, Roxbury, Somerville or Medford, and they left Harvard after four years without getting to know anybody. But Kennedy, whose family was quite comfortable financially, roomed in the College Yard and knew everybody. A close friend of Bob Fisher, the football hero of the day, he mixed socially with outstanding undergraduates, played first base on the baseball team, was elected to Hasty Pudding and the Dickey and the D.U. club.

When it came to earning a living after college, Kennedy continued to move out of his class in an occupation where his Celtic name and church marked him as a stranger. Anti-Irish Catholicism was as strong, perhaps stronger, in Boston economically as it was socially. James M. Curley has pointed out that Boston has had more than its share of skilled Irish politicians because around the turn of the century the fields of business and finance and most of the professions were barred to able young men of Irish descent; ward politics was one of the few avenues to opportunity left open to them. But just as Joe Kennedy had chosen Harvard, he chose banking. That meant dealing with State Street, the closed stronghold of the Adamses, the Lowells, the Cabots and the Forbeses. A few years after college and after serving an apprenticeship as a state bank examiner, Kennedy managed to gain control of the Columbia Trust Company in East Boston and became, at twenty-five, the youngest bank president in Massachusetts. The next step up was to become a utility company director. Twice the name of Kennedy was suggested as a member of the board of trustees of the Massachusetts Electric Company and twice he was turned down. Finally in 1917, around the time that Jack was born, he was made a trustee of the electric company. The company's president admitted to him that he had been rejected earlier only because he was an Irish Catholic, and apologized to him for the company's discrimination. The election caused a stir on State Street, somewhat like the one Jackie

Robinson created by becoming the first Negro to break into organized baseball.

After he broke through the barrier, Kennedy was helped onward and upward by two good Yankee friends, Guy Currier and Galen Stone. Currier recommended Kennedy to Charles M. Schwab for a top executive post at Bethlehem Steel's huge Fore River shipbuilding plant during World War I. Stone brought him into the managership of the Boston office of the Hayden Stone investment house after the war. But in Boston Kennedy was always rankled by the feeling of never really belonging, always conscious of that difference in race and religion that made him an oddity on State Street. And State Street was too narrow for him. In order to go where he had to go in order to show those people who had opposed his election to the utility trusteeship, he needed the faster and bigger action on Wall Street. Through his sons, Kennedy is still showing them. There is a connection between the trouble he had getting into the Massachusetts Electric Company and Jack's overpowering urge to beat the train to the crossing.

3

FRUIT IN THE HOUSE AND NOBODY SICK

As Joe Kennedy says, politics should come natural to his sons because both of their grandfathers, Patrick J. Kennedy and John F. ("Honey Fitz") Fitzgerald, were powerful Democratic politicians in Boston, where they were born of Irish parents who came to Massachusetts in the great wave of immigration after the potato famine of 1847. Pat Kennedy controlled the vote at the turn of the century in East Boston, where he is remembered warmly as a generous, kind and quiet-mannered man, quite unlike his more hot-tempered and outspoken multimillionaire son. The elder Kennedy and Fitzgerald, ward leader in the North End of the South End and Joseph J. Corbett of Charlestown, of of the South End and, Joseph J. Corbett of Charlestown, of the "Board of Strategy" which met in Room 8 of the Quincy House on Brattle Street near Scollay Square to select candidates for the Boston elections. They often had trouble with the famed Martin Lomasney, the iron dictator of Ward Eight in the West End where as many as sixty voters were sometimes registered from the address of one six-room lodging house. Lomasney once said to an office seeker, "I won't give you the whole of my ward but I'll give you three precincts, which means you'll get one thousand of my votes." In 1898 Lomasney had a pitched battle with Pat Kennedy and the Board of Strategy for control of the city's Democratic nominating convention, which Kennedy had placed at the Maverick House in his own East Boston. Kennedy stationed road blocks on the streets leading into East Boston to prevent Lomasney's delegates from attending the convention. But Lomasney passed through the barriers safely by disguising his entourage as a funeral procession, with several of his henchmen hidden inside the hearse. It was a political era rich in such incidents. A favorite dodge on the night before an election was to pound on tenement doors long after bedtime and then to urge the angry awakened occupants to vote on the morrow for the rival candidate. There was also the trick of "going over the ballot with a fine tooth comb." Ward heelers would pass out to voters a comb with its teeth carefully removed in certain places. When the comb was placed on the ballot, the gaps would show the names of the approved candidates.

Some of Joe Kennedy's biographies depict him as fighting his way up from the slums, but, like his wife, Rose Fitzgerald, he actually came from a lace curtain Irish family, which means, in Boston, a family that has fruit in the house when nobody is sick. Pat Kennedy owned three saloons, a wholesale liquor concern and a coal company and had an interest in the Columbia Trust Company where Joe later made his start in the banking business. Pat's wife, Mary Hickey, came from a substantial family. One of her brothers, Charles, was mayor of Brockton, Massachusetts, and another one, John, was a doctor in Winthrop. Joe Kennedy was also regarded with awe by other children in East Boston because a third uncle, Jim Hickey, was a local police captain. The Kennedys lived in a handsome spacious Colonial house at 165 Webster Street, on top of a hill overlooking Boston Harbor, which was torn down, while Joe was in Harvard, to make way for the Samuel Adams School. Later they moved to nearby Winthrop.

Joe was the oldest of four children; he had two younger sisters and a brother who died as a small boy. He showed business acumen at an early age, selling candy and fruit on excursion boats that were chartered for political outings. When he was fifteen, he organized a neighborhood baseball team named The Assumptions, after the Catholic church that its players attended, and raised money to outfit the team with white uniforms, embellished on the chest with an Old English letter "Ah," blue stockings and spiked shoes. After he found that the Assumptions played good enough baseball to attract sizeable crowds of spectators, Joe hired the enclosed Locust Street Park for a substantial rental fee and sold enough tickets to the games to end up the season with a profit. Telling an interviewer in later years about the Assumptions, he said, "It seems to me that boys in those days were a little more enterprising than they are now. What fifteen-year-old boy today would hire a ball park?"

Pat Kennedy served for a while as a state senator, but he preferred to be a quiet, behind-the-scenes politician. His son's father-in-law, the peppery and jaunty John F. Fitzgerald, was just the opposite type; he loved to bask in the spotlight as a candidate. Honey Fitz also loved to sing "Sweet

Adeline" at public gatherings, an incurable habit for which he became quite famous far and wide. Jack Kennedy remembers one time when Grandfather Fitzgerald took him and his brother Joe to call upon President Franklin D. Roosevelt. When Roosevelt saw Fitzgerald, he threw out his arms and cried, "El Dulce Adelino!" It developed that Roosevelt had heard about Honey Fitz singing "Sweet Adeline" in Spanish during a vacation trip in South America. Fitzgerald in his later years—he lived to be eighty-seven—made long speeches on the slightest provocation on the development of the Port of Boston or on the urgent need for all Bostonians to wear long woolen underwear so that the New England textile industry would be saved. On his birthday, or at any other time during the year when the spirit moved him, he would summon reporters to deliver lengthy statements on his views on world affairs, interspersed with reminiscences of the Boston fire of 1872, of listening as a boy to literary conversations of Ralph Waldo Emerson, Henry Wadsworth Longfellow and James Russell Lowell at the Old Corner Bookstore, of flying with Claude Graham-White, the British aviator, over Boston Harbor in 1911. When he learned of the death of Jacob Ruppert, Fitzgerald called the sports department of the *Boston Post* and talked steadily on the telephone for almost an hour about how he had persuaded Ruppert to buy the New York Yankees. Edwin O'Connor, author of *The Last Hurrah*, was walking one evening several years ago alone in the North End of Boston, in search of spaghetti and wine, when he came upon Fitzgerald on a side street. The little ex-mayor grabbed O'Connor's arm, quickly introduced himself, pointed to the nearby Faneuil Hall and began to recite its history. "Now come with me, young man, and I'll show you the house where I was born," Fitzgerald continued briskly. He led the way upstairs in a tenement house on Hanover Street, opened the door of a small apartment where an Italian family was preparing its dinner. "Good evening, Mrs. Genaro," he said to the housewife. "I am just showing this young man the house where I was born. Pay no attention to us." Then he took O'Connor through all the rooms, including the bedrooms, pointing out exactly where he slept as a child, where his parents slept and where he did his studying while attending Boston Latin School.

Fitzgerald had a curious political career. Just before his fifty-first birthday in 1914, when his daughter, Rose, married Joe Kennedy, he gave up his position as mayor of Boston. (James M. Curley once observed that Fitzgerald was the first mayor in the history of the City of Boston who did not have a beard or a mustache.) After he left City Hall, he continued to be an active figure in politics for almost thirty years, running twice for U.S. senator, twice for governor and once for the House of Representatives, but never again in all that time did he win another elective office. Figtzgerald's best fight (Boston politicians always refer to an election or primary race as a "fight"; they seldom use the word "campaign") was for the Senate against the supposedly unbeatable Republican incumbent, the elder Henry Cabot Lodge, in 1916. Honey Fitz shook Yankee Brahmin Boston to its heels by coming within 30,000 votes of upsetting Lodge. Sadly, Fitzgerald did not live quite long enough to enjoy the great day in 1952 when his grandson and namesake, John Fitzgerald Kennedy, defeated Lodge's grandson and namesake, the second Henry Cabot Lodge, in a similar battle for the same senate seat. John F. did play a noisy and active supporting role, however, in 1946 at the age of eighty-three in launching Jack as a politician, singing "Sweet Adeline" in behalf of his grandson's candidacy for Congress. In his day, Fitzgerald was a commanding figure on the Boston scene. Curley, no admirer of The Little General as he called Honey Fitz, tells in his entertaining autobiography, *I'd Do It Again!*, of conducting a class at his political and social Tammany Club in Roxbury in the fundamentals of American history and civics for Irish immigrants who were preparing for their citizenship tests. Curley asked one student who made the laws of the nation.

"John F. Fitzgerald," the man said.

Curley inquired about the source of the laws of Massachusetts.

"John F. Fitzgerald," the man repeated.

"Who is the President of the United States?" Curley asked.

"John F. Fitzgerald."

As late as the late Thirties, when Joseph P. Kennedy had gained national and international fame as a New Deal administrator and Ambassador to Great Britain, the Boston newspapers continued to describe him as John F. Fitzgerald's son-in-law.

Like her father, Rose Fitzgerald was born in the North End, one of the politician's six children. Her mother,

Josephine Mary Hannon, was a girl from the rural community of South Acton, where John F. had met her on a North End political club's berry-picking outing. In 1904, when Rose was still a small girl, the Fitzgeralds moved to a larger and more fashionable home at 39 Welles Avenue near Codman Square in Dorchester, where Honey Fitz as mayor entertained such celebrities as Sir Thomas Lipton and the Japanese Admiral Togo. A few years later, when Rose was attending Dorchester High School, she began to keep company on the quiet with Joe Kennedy, who was then a big man at Boston Latin School—president of his class, colonel of the school's military cadet regiment, manager of the football team, baseball captain, and, incidentally, winner of a Boston high school batting championship trophy which had been donated by John F. Fitzgerald. Boston Latin, then as now, was academically one of the most rigorous preparatory schools in the nation and Joe was never much of a student. He was continually in scholastic hot water. But, as one of his classmates recalled in later years, he had a knack when he was summoned to the principal's office of turning a dressing-down into a pleasant social call.

Because their fathers were closely associated politically, the Fitzgeralds and the Kennedys had known each other for years. They had spent one summer together at the Everett House at Old Orchard Beach in Maine when Rose and Joe were children. "We went steady for seven years before we were married," Joe said recently, "but going steady in those days was a different proposition from the way kids go steady today. During that time Rose went to the Sacred Heart Academy in New York and then to a convent school in Europe. And I was busy with other things—going to Harvard, playing baseball for the Bethlehem ball team in the White Mountain semi-pro league for a few summers, and then running a sightseeing bus in partenership with another fellow. But I was never seriously interested in anyone else."

A girlhood friend of Rose's says that her romantic interest in the Kennedy boy had to be kept more or less undercover because John F. Fitzgerald was not too keen about having Joe as a son-in-law at that time. He was more partial toward a wealthy contractor. It was also said in Boston that Sir Thomas Lipton had his eye on the mayor's stunning daughter. In that second decade of the century, an Irish

Catholic girl with Rose's genteel Sacred Heart convent training in New York and Holland was quite unusual in Boston.
She organized the Ace of Clubs, originally a group of cul-
ture-minded Boston Irish young ladies who attempted,
without much success, to conduct their early meetings in
French.

Any doubts that John F. Fitzgerald might have had about
the qualifications of Joe Kennedy as a son-in-law must have
been dispelled in January, 1914, when Joe became, at
twenty-five, the youngest bank president in Massachusetts,
and possibly in the entire United States. Kennedy later told
John B. Kennedy, who interviewed him in 1928 for one of
those success stories in the old *American Magazine*, that he
decided on going into banking after Harvard because he
wanted to start at the bottom of a ladder that had more
than one rung. "I knew banking could lead a man anywhere,
as it played an important part in every business," Kennedy
said to Kennedy. Joe began his study of banking by passing
a civil service examination and getting a job with the state
as a bank examiner at $1,500 a year. He stayed at the job
for two years, learning a lot and finding it fascinating.
According to the *American Magazine's* version of Joe's
climb to success, he awoke one morning to find himself
being called to a meeting of the directors of the Columbia
Trust Company in East Boston who offered him the position
of bank president, bang, just like that. Actually it was not
that quick and simple.

The Columbia Trust Company, a neighborhood institution
in which Pat Kennedy had an interest, was in danger of being swallowed up by a rival savings bank. Learning of the
situation, Joe dug up $45,000 in loans from various people
who had a sentimental interest in the Columbia Trust,
tained his ownership of the trust company until the late
of the company and made himself its president. Kennedy re-
trained his ownership of the trust company until the late
1940s' when he sold it to one of the Boston banks. As a
part of their education, each of his three older sons worked
in the bank for two weeks of one of their summer vacations
from college. Bobby liked the bank work so well that he
stayed on for an extra two weeks. One of his duties was to
collect rents in the crowded East Boston tenement buildings
that the bank had taken over in mortgage foreclosures. He
came home wide-eyed to tell his mother and sisters how large

poorer families lived in three or four rooms and slept on the fire escapes on hot summer nights.

Shortly after he became a bank president, still strapped financially from raising the $45,000, Joe borrowed another $2,000 for a down payment on a $6,500 house on Beals Street in Brookline. That October, in 1914, he and Rose Fitzgerald were married by Cardinal O'Connell in a splendid wedding ceremony. They went to the Greenbrier at White Sulphur Springs for their honeymoon.

In July of the next year, Young Joe was born at the Fitzgerald's summer house at Hull, Massachusetts, and Jack was born at the Brookline house on May 29, 1917. Shortly after Jack's birth, his father turned over the management of the East Boston bank to Pat Kennedy and accepted Charles M. Schwab's offer of the job as second in command, under Joseph W. Powell, at Bethlehem Steel's big Fore River ship-building plant in Quincy. One of the first things Joe Kennedy noticed in Fore River was the lack of eating facilities for the 22,000 workers at the booming, war-production swollen shipyard. He lost no time putting into operation as a profitable sideline a big cafeteria where lunches were sold.

As a production executive at Fore River, Kennedy became acquainted with Franklin D. Roosevelt, then Assistant Secretary of the Navy. Representing the government in dealings with Bethlehem Steel's ship builders, Roosevelt was often embroiled in battles with Kennedy. At one time they argued about vessels that Bethlehem Steel refused to deliver to the Argentine government, as Roosevelt requested, until all bills for the construction had been paid. Roosevelt's attempts to arbitrate the matter got nowhere and finally, losing his patience, he told Kennedy that he was sending Navy tugboats to Fore River at two o'clock the following afternoon to tow the ships away, which he did.

At the end of World War I, when government-ordered production at Fore River began to slacken, Kennedy decided to try to sell ships to Galen Stone, the investment banker who owned a controlling interest in a large commercial shipping line. Finding it difficult to arrange an appointment with Stone, Kennedy found out when he was making a trip from Boston to New York, took the same train, sat beside him, and gave him a sales talk. Stone bought no ships but he became so interested in Kennedy that he offered him a job with Hayden Stone that Kennedy promptly accepted.

Kennedy was never a man to stick long in one job; he

could always see something more attractive on the horizon. As manager of Hayden Stone's Boston office, he saw the beginning of the wild financial boom of the Twenties and itched to get into it as a lone wolf independent operator on Wall Street. Still in his early thirties and now the father of five children—Young Joe and Jack had been quickly followed by three daughters, Rosemary, Kathleen and Eunice—he surprised his Yankee associates on State Street by throwing up his position with Hayden Stone to free-lance as a financier and stock speculator. His Boston Latin School year book's class prophecy had predicted that he would earn his living "in a very roundabout way," which is a fair enough description of how he reaped a fortune in the secretive and unrestricted stock market of the free and easy Calvin Coolidge administration. On Wall Street, Kennedy became a master of the art of managing pools; in partnership with a few other speculators he would take options on, say, fifty thousand shares of a cheap, idle and unnoticed stock and then stir up interest in it on the exchange by the Wall Street practice known as "window dressing"—buying and selling small lots of the stock here and there around the country in order to get its name mentioned frequently on the ticker tape. "You simply advertised the stock by trading it," he says. Seeing this deceptive action, suckers would assume that something was up. They would rush to buy the stock, sending its price up a few points. Then the pool operators would sell their shares, pocket the profit, and go whistling on their merry way.

In 1933, just before Kennedy in a dramatic turnabout organized, at President Roosevelt's request, the Securities and Exchange Commission that outlawed those very practices, he managed one such pool with Libby-Owens-Ford glass stock that was later investigated by Ferdinand Pecora's Senate banking and currency committee because it cleaned up such a notorious profit. The gravy was estimated at around $395,000 but Kennedy has intimated since then that it was actually much higher. The price of the Libby-Owens-Ford stock was pushed up for the killing by the repeal of prohibition. Rumors were spread in the market that the glass company was about to earn big money by going into the liquor bottle business. Disappointed buyers of the stock found out later that Libby-Owens-Ford had no intention of making bottles.

Recently Kennedy talked about his first big experience

as a Wall Street stock manipulator, an incident that illustrates the skill and driving energy that later made him one of the world's wealthiest contemporary self-made men and which also throws light on the consuming Kennedy competitive urge. In 1924, when he was still living in Brookline, but in a larger and nicer house on Naples Road, he was awakened late one night by somebody ringing the bell at his front door. Coming downstairs with a robe thrown over his pajamas, he found that the caller was Walter Howey, the colorful Hearst newspaper editor, the original model on whom Charles MacArthur and Ben Hecht based the wild and hard-boiled managing editor, Walter Burns, in their play, *The Front Page*. Howey had lately been transferred from Chicago, where he worked with MacArthur and Hecht, to the editorship of Hearst's *Boston American*. He had put a ban on political news, a peculiar move for a newspaper because in Boston politics is a bigger topic of reader interest than baseball or sex. John F. Fitzgerald was running for governor at the time. Kennedy went to Howey, pointing out to him that his disapproval of political coverage was unwise, and persuaded him to give Fitzgerald generous publicity in the *Boston American*. In return, Kennedy invited Howey to feel free to call upon him if he ever needed help or advice with his financial affairs.

Howey was now anxiously in need of Kennedy's assistance. In his Chicago days, the newspaper editor had become a close friend of John Hertz and had bought heavily in the stock of Hertz's Yellow Cab Company. A month before Hertz had listed Yellow Cab on the New York Stock Exchange without taking the precaution of hiring an expert on Wall Street to watch over the stock and protect it. For some reason or other that Hertz and his associates were not able to figure, rivals were using a New York brokerage firm to do a destructive job on the stock. Heavy sales from that firm had driven it down from 85 to 50 and it was about to drop lower. Hertz had heard about Kennedy and knew of his friendship with Howey. He wanted Kennedy to go to New York and wage a counter battle to stop the stock's headlong decline and to save the corporation. Kennedy was ill with neuritis at the time and his wife was expecting, within two weeks, the birth of their sixth child, Patricia. But Kennedy packed a bag, and caught the next train to New York.

"I took a room at the old Waldorf Astoria and went to bed right away because I was too sick to stand up," he said while recalling it a short time ago. "Hertz came to see me. I told him I'd need five million dollars right away to play around with. He went back to his friends in Chicago, Albert Lasker and Phil Wrigley, and raised the money. By then the stock was down to 48. I had some wires put into the room and a ticker tape machine, and, lying there in bed, sick, I got on the telephones and went to work."

Buying here and selling there, in widely separated parts of the country, in secret and strange maneuvers that had the opposing brokers on the floor of the stock exchange scratching their heads in wonder, Kennedy juggled Yellow Cab from his sick bed in the hotel room so that the stock went up in a few weeks from 48 to 62. Then it dropped again, first to 50 and then to 46. After several more days of frantic figuring and manipulation, it rose again to 51 and there at last it stayed firm, with its descent halted and Hertz's five million dollars still intact.

"I woke up one morning, exhausted, and I realized that I hadn't been out of that hotel room in seven weeks," he said. "My baby, Pat, had been born and was almost a month old, and I hadn't even seen her."

It was also during the Twenties, while he was trading on Wall Street, that Kennedy took a memorable flyer in the movie and theater business. He started probing into the entertainment field by buying a chain of New England movie houses, part of which he still owns. Then he became interested in the Film Booking Offices of America, which was not merely a booking agency, as its name implied, but also a Hollywood production company. Owned by a British banking syndicate, FBO was in bad shape from mismanagement. Kennedy raised money and went to London, making the British an offer for the company which has variously been reported as low as one million dollars and as high as ten millions. Among the many legendary tales told about Kennedy in Boston is one that says he found himself sitting near the Prince of Wales, now the Duke of Windsor, in a London restaurant during that business trip and struck up a casual conversation with the Prince. During the talk, Kennedy mentioned that he was having a hard time trying to see a certain banker in the syndicate controlling FBO. The next day an unsolicited letter of introduction for Kennedy, signed by the Prince, was said to have been delivered to his hotel, opening all doors in London to him. Kennedy now says with a smile that he does not recall the incident, but, in any case, on February 24, 1926, he bought FBO and took over the management of the company.

Kennedy quickly turned FBO into a money maker by cutting costs and putting into the running of the company simple and sensible procedures observed by all other businesses but unknown in Hollywood at that time. "Employees in moving picture companies were vastly overpaid," he said to an interviewer while explaining his success with FBO. "I found that an accountant, for example, whose pay in any other industry would range from $5,000 to $10,000, was getting $20,000 in Hollywood. I changed that." More important was Kennedy's policy of avoiding competition with the major studios that were producing expensive pictures for the lavish movie palaces on Times Square in New York and on The Loop in Chicago. He made FBO profitable by concentrating on inexpensive films for small town theaters. The company specialized in grinding out Fred Thomson cowboy thrillers, costing $30,000 each, at the rate of one movie a week. The bigger studios then were spending $300,000 on an average picture. Kennedy enjoys recalling one time when he was unable to make up his mind about hiring Red Grange, the football star, for a leading role in a college football movie. Grange had been turned down by several larger producers. Kennedy asked his young sons, Joe and Jack, if they would like to see Grange in a movie and they gave him a immediate and violent shout of yes. Kennedy signed up the gridiron hero and the picture starring him turned out to be highly profitable.

In Hollywood, Kennedy was introduced to Marcus Loew as a banker from Boston. "A banker?" Loew said. "I thought nobody went into the movie business except furriers." Loew and the other founding fathers of the cinema industry were subsequently astounded by the Boston banker's sudden rise from his modest foothold at FBO to the top peaks of the moving picture and theater world along a winding, meteoric trail that is difficult to trace. And then, also like a meteor, he quickly disappeared and made a fast exit back to Wall Street. After putting FBO on a sound, money-making basis, Kennedy sold an interest in the company one noon in a conversation with David Sarnoff at a New York oyster bar. Sarnoff's Radio Corporation of America was glad to get into FBO because it needed an outlet for its moving picture sound patents and talking pictures were the coming thing at the time. Then Kennedy sold another piece of FBO to

E. F. Albee's Keith-Albee-Orpheum theater and vaudeville chain. At the same time, he became chairman of Pathé, another film company and distributing agency. In partnership with his friend Elisha Walker of the Transamerica banking group and with J. J. Murdock of the Albee organization, he jostled Albee aside and got control of Keith-Albee-Orpheum, which, in turn, he merged with FBO. The merged motion picture and theater and vaudeville concerns were then sold to RCA, becoming the radio corporation's show business subsidiary, Radio Keith Orpheum, better known as RKO. For a period of five months during these involved negotiations, Kennedy was drawing three weekly pay checks of $2,000 each in his positions as head of FBO, Keith-Albee-Orpheum and Pathé and he also managed to find the time within those same five months to serve as a special adviser to still one more movie company, First National, for a fee of $12,500 a month.

When he disposed of FBO and Keith-Albee-Orpheum and gave up the task of advising First National, Kennedy was left with only his chairmanship of Pathé. To occupy some of the resulting idleness, he turned to independent production of supercolossal film epics starring Gloria Swanson. This was an experience he would rather forget.

The first Kennedy-Swanson picture was the famous unfinished *Queen Kelly*, which is still talked about in Hollywood. It was originally written and directed by the moody Erich von Stroheim. Kennedy and Miss Swanson made the error of starting work on the movie before von Stroheim had figured out an ending for it. The noted German contended later that the filming had gone smoothly until one day on the set when Miss Swanson said to him, "Excuse me, I've got to make a phone call," and was never seen again.

Kennedy and Miss Swanson felt that the story von Stroheim was filming bore no resemblance to the partly completed script they had seen and approved. Gloria found herself playing a convent-educated girl who is seduced by a Prussian army officer and then chased from a palace in her nightgown by an indignant queen who is in love with the army officer herself. It was then that Miss Swanson decided to ask von Stroheim what would come next. He explained that the ravished convent school girl, whose name was Kitty Kelly, would go to German East Africa to receive an inheritance from a recently deceased aunt whom she had never seen. The inheritance would turn out to be a string of bawdy houses. The writer-director also mentioned a stirring flashback sequence that he had in mind, showing the bordello madam on her deathbed receiving the last rites of the Roman Catholic Church from an admiring young priest. That was when Miss Swanson excused herself to make the telephone call. She called Kennedy at his home in Palm Beach and told him that the picture would have to be stopped. "There's a madman in charge," she is reported to have said to him.

More than $750,000 had already been spent on the picture. Kennedy fired von Stroheim, hired on the advice of Irving Thalberg another director, Edmund Goulding, and spent another $100,00 but nobody could work out an ending for what von Stroheim had already filmed. Instead, Goulding made another Swanson picture, *The Trespasser*, that broke box office records and recouped the losses of *Queen Kelly*. By then, Kennedy had had enough of the moving picture business. Five million dollars richer, but thirty-five pounds under his normal weight, he was glad to get back to the peace and quiet of Wall Street.

4

I'M FOR ROOSEVELT

UNLIKE H. M. Pulham, Esquire, and other heroes in the novels of John P. Marquand, Joe Kennedy felt no qualms and no restraining ties when he moved from Boston to New York in 1926. He was glad to go; he had just taken over FBO, which had its main offices in Manhattan, and his other financial interests were centered on Wall Street; but mainly, as he has often said since, he wanted his children to grow up in social atmosphere that was not dominated by the proper Bostonian Yankees. "They wouldn't have asked my daughters to join their debutante clubs," he said recently. "Not that our girls would have joined anyway—they never gave two cents for that society stuff. But the point is they wouldn't have been asked in Boston." For a multimillionaire's daughters, all of the Kennedy girls have been singularly uninterested in high society life. When Kathleen was in London in 1938, she was formally presented to British society at a dinner and reception but that was a necessary formality because of her father's position as U.S. Ambassador. She and her sisters never had coming-out parties in this country and seldom appeared at fancy social events in New York. A friend of the Kennedys was asked not long ago if the family seemed snooty or high-toned. "Well, let us take Eunice, for example," he said. "One time Eunice was flying home from Europe. To save the extra charge for a berth, she spread her mink coat out in the aisle, stretched out on it and went to sleep. Every time I've seen Eunice at Hyannis Port she has been wearing her brothers' sneakers."

Kennedy made his departure from Boston in splendor, packing his children and household servants into a private railroad car, at a siding near their house in Brookline, and carrying them directly to Riverdale where he had bought a new home. There were then seven children. Bobby, a year old, was the youngest. A few years later, after Jean and Teddy were born, the family was living in a red brick eleven-bedroom mansion in the Westchester County suburb of Bronxville, which they kept until World War II. Every summer they returned to Massachusetts, but Hyannis Port is not Boston; most of their neighbors at the Cape Cod place were other summer residents from New York and Pittsburgh. When Young Joe and Jack were at Choate School, the Kennedys acquired the Palm Beach house where they have gathered together every Christmas since then.

If anybody in the family was reluctant to leave Boston, it was Rose Kennedy who is closely attached to her family there and whose only intimate friends over the years are a few Boston women whom she has known since girlhood. A quiet, retiring woman with none of the supercharged energy and drive that her husband has passed on to her children, and with a sharper interest in Paris fashions than any of her daughters, Rose, as one of Jack's friends puts it, runs on a different track from the rest of the Kennedys. Last year she confided to friends that she was unable to understand why Jack wanted to run for President. "After all, he could stay in the Senate and have a nice, interesting life," she said. One of her closest woman companions says of her, "If I tried to tell you how kind and gentle Rose Kennedy is, you wouldn't believe it. In all the years I've known her, I've never heard her say an unkind word about anybody, and how many women are like that? I remember one time playing bridge with her when that hot news about King Edward and Wally Simpson was beginning to be passed around. One of the girls at the table brought it up. Rose stopped her and said she wouldn't have it discussed in her house because it was slander. I never saw a mother with such devotion to her children. When they had the house in Bronxville decorated by Elsie De Wolfe, Rose's room was furnished with pieces that had a very beautiful but very delicate and fragile silk upholstery. Rose took one look at it and had it covered up immediately with rough, hard slip covers. She said the room was no good to her unless the smaller children could play in it with her. This great closeness that the Kennedys have as a family unit is entirely due to Rose."

As youngsters in school together at Dexter in Brookline, at Riverdale Country Day and Choate, Young Joe, the star of the family, overshadowed the more frail and often sickly Jack. "Jack turned out to be our most intellectual member of the family because he wasn't strong enough as a kid to go in for athletics as much as Joe and the other boys," his sister, Jean, says. At Choate, Joe was awarded the Harvard Trophy for being the football player who best combined scholarship and sportsmanship, which seemed to Jack, at the time, bigger than a Nobel prize. Joe was an outstanding skipper in sailing races at Cape Cod, giving orders to Jack who served as his crew. A friend recalls visiting them one stormy day in Hyannis Port when they were to compete in interclub races. The visiting sailors and the yacht club officials agreed that the wind and the water were too rough for racing but the Kennedys insisted on going through with the regatta. "Come on, let's show them it's all right," Joe said to Jack. The two boys jumped into their boat, ran up the sail and headed out to sea. A few hundred yards from the dock, they both fell overboard. The startled watchers were about to go to their rescue when Joe, and then Jack, swam through the waves to the empty sailboat and climbed back into it. "See what we did?" Joe said when they returned, dripping wet, to the dock. "That ought to prove it's safe enough out there for the race." The Kennedys were overruled, however, and the race was postponed.

Young Joe also gave orders to Jack at home, or tried to. "Jack and Joe used to fight a lot as boys," Bobby told a *Life* magazine reporter a few years ago, "but I was nine years younger so I escaped that." As the oldest of the nine Kennedy children, Young Joe took it upon himself to act as the first sergeant of the family. Looking back on it later, Jack wrote respectfully in *As We Remember Joe*, the privately published book of memories that he compiled after his brother's death, "Joe made the task of bringing up a large family immeasurably easier for my father and mother, for what they taught him he passed on to us and their teachings were not diluted through him but strengthened." But as a teen-ager, only two years younger than Joe, Jack often found his passing on of parental guidance rather hard to take. At that time, during the Thirties, Young Joe often acted the role of the man in the house because Old Joe was frequently in Washington working for Franklin D. Roosevelt.

Kennedy climbed on Roosevelt's bandwagon long before the 1932 Democratic convention. A *New York Times* news story on May 8 of that year reported that Roosevelt, vacationing at Warm Springs, entertained Kennedy and his aide and right hand man, Eddie Moore, together with John F. Fitzgerald and James M. Curley, at a picnic at

Pine Mountain Woods. The talk at the picnic must have been largely concerned with Massachusetts, where Curley was one of the few Roosevelt backers at that stage of the campaign; the rest of the state's Democrats were still for Al Smith. Barred from the Massachusetts delegation because he was pro-Roosevelt, the always resourceful Curley turned up on the floor at Chicago as chairman of the Puerto Rican delegation and arose to cast that island's six votes for F.D.R. The *Times* reporter covering the Warm Springs picnic also noted that Kennedy had just visited in California his close friend, William Randolph Hearst. At the convention two months later, it was Hearst's influence that switched California's crucial forty-four votes from John Nance Garner to Roosevelt, breaking a deadlock between Roosevelt and Smith.

It seemed curious for a conservative, wealthy Wall Streeter like Kennedy to be backing Roosevelt. Four years later, when Roosevelt was running for re-election against Alfred M. Landon, Kennedy wrote a widely quoted book entitled *I'm for Roosevelt*, in which he explained why he supported the New York governor against Hoover in 1932 and why he felt that the New Deal's recovery measures were saving the country's economic structure. Joseph Medill Patterson's New York *Daily News*, then strongly pro-Roosevelt, called the book "a masterpiece." "Mr. Kennedy's book is the best answer we have yet seen to those who blindly hate President Roosevelt for having saved their shirts and possibly their skins for them," the *Daily News* said.

In *I'm for Roosevelt*, Kennedy said that as a father of nine children he was deeply worried during the depression years of 1931 and 1932 about the future economic security of his family. He decided that he would gladly give up half of all his wealth if by making such a sacrifice he could be given a definite assurance that the other half of his possessions would be safeguarded in the years to come. He said that he mentioned this feeling to friends in his financial bracket and most of them agreed that they, too, would give up half of what they had if they could be sure of keeping the other half. "That will give you an idea of how shaky the country seemed to us in those days," Kennedy said, in a more recent discussion of his reasons for supporting Roosevelt. "Long before the stock market crash, back at the peak of the boom, when Jack was nine or ten years old, I had established million dollar trust funds for each of our children.

After the crash, I began to wonder if those trust funds were going to be worth a damn. I was really worried. I knew that big, drastic changes had to be made in our economic system and I felt that Roosevelt was the one who could make those changes. I wanted him in the White House for my own security, and for the security of our kids, and I was ready to do anything to help elect him." More cynical observers have said that Kennedy supported Roosevelt only because he knew that F.D.R. would be the winner.

Kennedy himself had survived the 1929 stock market crash without serious injury, a survival which must be regarded as one of the major accomplishments of his Wall Street career. It has often been said and occasionally written that he cleaned up $15,000,000 in a few hours during the crash by selling short, but people who know Wall Street point out that it was practically impossible at any time in those dark days when all stocks were falling steadily to sell short for a profit. The big trick was to keep from losing money. In any case, as worried as he was about his money in 1932, Kennedy still had enough of it to be able to afford an outright donation of $25,000 and a loan of another $50,-000 to Roosevelt's campaign fund. He personally raised an additional $100,000 from friends and joined the campaign staff in a full-time job as financial chairman and fund raiser, sharing a compartment with Raymond Moley, the candidate's chief speech writer and policy adviser, on the Roosevelt barnstorming train. Reporters covering the cross-country campaign tour wrote that Kennedy avoided the speech-making rallies and political dinners where Roosevelt appeared at the various stops, to wander off by himself and to talk with townspeople about the election in barber shops and cafeterias.

After the election of Roosevelt, Kennedy was mentioned as a possible cabinet member. It was reported that the President-elect considered him as Secretary of the Treasury and then decided to appoint him Secretary of Commerce, but that the crotchety Louis McHenry Howe, Roosevelt's secretary, disliked Kennedy and kept him out of the Commerce post. So when Roosevelt went into the White House, Kennedy was left empty-handed. But although he did not get a job out of it immediately, his work in the campaign was well remembered by Roosevelt and won him warm admirers in Roosevelt's inner circle—Moley, the head brain-truster of that first New Deal regime, Marguerite ("Missy")

Le Hand and Grace Tully, the President's secretaries, and son James. Besides, Kennedy had other things to occupy his time. The repeal of prohibition was coming. It was in that summer of 1933, after Roosevelt took office, that Joe managed the lucrative pool in Libby-Owens-Ford glass stock and organized a liquor importing company, Somerset Importers, Ltd., for which he obtained large permits for bringing liquor into the country. That September, Joe and Rose made a trip to Europe with Jimmy and Betsy Cushing Roosevelt and came back with a deal that made Somerset the U.S. agents for Haig and Haig, King William and John Dewar Scotch whiskeys and for Gordon's gin. Five years later, when Kennedy was Ambassador to the Court of St. James, the *Saturday Evening Post* published a caustic article about Jimmy Roosevelt, written by the late Alva Johnston, which contended that the President's son had introduced Kennedy, in London in 1933, to the British distillers who controlled the Scotch whiskeys. Because his government permits enabled him to import big quantities of Scotch and gin for "medical purposes" before the prohibition law was repealed, Kennedy was able to have his Somerset warehouses filled to the brim with Haig and Haig and Dewar's when the United States went wet and opened its bars.

When Johnston's *Saturday Evening Post* article was published, Kennedy heatedly denied that it was Jimmy Roosevelt who put him into the liquor business. He said to reporters, "Kennedy was doing all right by himself before he ever met Jimmy Roosevelt." Last year a friend of Joe was speculating about the reasons for Eleanor Roosevelt's outspoken opposition to Jack Kennedy and her remark in her column about Joe spending large sums of money to put his son in the White House. "I suspect it may go back to that time when Jimmy Roosevelt helped Joe with that Scotch whiskey deal," Kennedy's friend said. "Maybe Jimmy thought he and Joe were going to be partners. If so, he soon found out that when Joe Kennedy is starting a business he doesn't have partners."

At the time that prohibition was repealed, Roosevelt's outstanding young brain trusters, Benjamin Cohen, James M. Landis and Thomas G. Corcoran were preparing a bill for Congress that would impose federal regulation on Wall Street. This legislative measure was the direct result of Ferdinand Pecora's memorable Senate Banking and Currency

Committee investigation of demoralizing stock exchange practices that had led to the 1929 crash, the hearings at which the embarrassed J. P. Morgan posed for the famous newspaper picture with the lady midget on his lap. The stock exchange bill aroused a storm of opposition from big business and finance tycoons, under the leadership of Richard Whitney, president of the New York Stock Exchange, who was later to serve a sentence in Sing Sing for fraud. As Will Rogers wrote, "Those old Wall Street boys are putting up an awful fight to keep the government from putting a cop on their corner." Sam Rayburn said that the bill was battled by "the most powerful lobby ever organized against any bill which ever came up in Congress."

The Securities Exchange Act, as the bill was called, aimed to make Wall Street a clearing house for regulated business investments instead of a gambling mart. It outlawed wild buying on margin, one of the main causes of so many wiped-out savings accounts in 1929, and it protected investors from secret manipulations of the bigger behind-the-scenes operators—pools, rigging of market prices, options, washed sales, matched orders. It was passed after long debates and revisions, and a five-man commission, to be known as the Securities and Exchange Commission, was established by Congress to administer both the exchange act and the earlier Securities Act of 1933. On the suggestion of Raymond Moley, Roosevelt made Joe Kennedy the chairman of the commission. This appointment caused almost as much indignation among the New Deal liberals as the original proposal of the act had stirred up among big business men and industrialists. Having put a police force on Wall Street, the economic reformers assumed that one of their own men, Landis or Pecora, would be its chief. When John T. Flynn, Pecora's right hand in the original Wall Street investigation, heard that Kennedy, a notorious stock exchange manipulator himself, was to head the commission, he wrote, "I say it isn't true. It is impossible. It could not happen." Roy Howard, publisher of the Scripps-Howard newspapers, went to the White House personally to protest against Kennedy's appointment. It seemed like appointing Jimmy Walker to clean up New York's City Hall. But, as he explained to his cabinet, Roosevelt reasoned that a man like Kennedy who knew Wall Street from the inside was better qualified to put a clamp on its shady practices. Roosevelt also wanted to reassure the stock exchange that the commission was not out to strangle investment activity with Communist-like theories, as so many Republicans and business men were charging. He felt that Kennedy could persuade the Wall Streeters to accept federal regulation with less resistance than a Harvard Law School intellectual might encounter. To placate the New Dealers, Roosevelt filled the other four places on the commission with liberal-minded economic experts, Landis, Pecora, George C. Mathews and Robert Healy, who were untainted by Wall Street wealth. Moley recalled later, in writing about the New Deal, that when he mentioned the Securities and Exchange Commission appointments to Tom Corcoran, the young braintruster said, after complaining about Kennedy, "Oh, well, we've got four out of five anyhow." Moley asked indignantly what he meant. "What I mean is that four are for us and one is for business," Moley quoted Corcoran as saying.

But under Kennedy's direction, the Securities and Exchange Commission became in its first critical year a great popular success. It was, in fact, the only economic reform of the Roosevelt administration that won unanimous praise from liberals and conservatives alike. As Kennedy's role in launching the securities and exchange regulations was described by Arthur M. Schlesinger, Jr., in *The Coming of the New Deal,* "he achieved the acceptance of SEC without sacrifice of principle and he had given its administrative operations invaluable momentum." The stock exchange people and the country's investors, Schlesinger goes on to say, soon found that the new laws "removed the whole process of capital investment from the realm of guess and gamble and rested it—through the detailed and continuous disclosure required by the SEC—on the solid basis of reliable fact . . . In a short time, few men on Wall Street would wish the repeal of this legislation which, when proposed, they had so desperately resisted."

While winning over Wall Street to the SEC's ideas, Kennedy also won over many of the Roosevelt cohorts who had deplored his appointment to the chairmanship. They found that he could get along smoothly with Jim Landis, Justice Brandeis' protégé who had been brought to Washington from Harvard Law School by Felix Frankfurter. Kennedy and Landis saw eye-to-eye on the problems of toughening up the SEC laws and they brought William O. Douglas, then a Yale corporation law professor, into the commission to work out a whole new reorganization of the stock exchange. After serving a year as the commission's chairman, in which time, working long hours and weekends, he secured Wall Street's acceptance of the new trading rules and stirred up financing activity in those new channels, Kennedy resigned and Landis took over his position. Two years later, when Landis became dean of Harvard Law School, Douglas became the commission's chairman. From there, Roosevelt appointed him a justice of the Supreme Court. Landis and Douglas have remained close to Kennedy. Now in private practice as a New York lawyer, Landis is Kennedy's legal adviser. He occupies an office near Kennedy's office in the Kennedy-owned building at 230 Park Avenue, next to Grand Central Terminal, and spends much of his time working on legislative matters for Jack Kennedy.

Joe Kennedy's success as the launcher of the Securities and Exchange Commission made his stock soar in the White House. Columnists began to refer to him and Jesse Jones as the only business men in Roosevelt's inner circle. In the year after he left the SEC, Kennedy wrote *I'm for Roosevelt* and worked for the President's 1936 re-election, picked up a $150,000 fee for drafting a reorganization plan for David Sarnoff's Radio Corporation of America and received $50,000 for telling Paramount Pictures why it was failing to make a profit in the movie business. His study of Paramount pointed out, among other things, that on the production of one picture no less than nineteen writers had been engaged in a desperate attempt to express one inarticulate producer's ideas. Roosevelt was soon after him to take on another hard job for the government, the organization of the Maritime Commission, which had been created by Congress in June, 1936, but which had still not reached the blueprint stage in March, 1937, when the President asked Kennedy to get it rolling.

The United States Merchant Marine fleet was in a sorry mess at that time and Kennedy was understandably reluctant to have any part of it. But Roosevelt broke down his resistance. "I can say no to that fellow on the telephone but face to face he gets me," he said about F.D.R. at the time. Kennedy finally agreed to take the Maritime Commission chairmanship under two conditions: first, he would not give up a number of stocks in his family's irrevocable trusts that conflicted with the interests of the maritime job, and, secondly, he would be relieved of the chairmanship as soon as he arranged the new subsidies called for by the

Maritime Act and started the commission functioning properly. Roosevelt quickly agreed to the second condition. Congress, which wanted Kennedy for the shipping cleanup task as urgently as the President did, promptly passed for the first time in its history a joint resolution excusing Kennedy from the law affecting his ownership of shipping and shipbuilding stocks.

That summer of 1937 was one that Kennedy does not care to remember. When Congress had passed the Maritime Act on June 29, 1936, it allowed a period of one year for the incredibly complicated, and in the opinion of many experts, apparently impossible, setting up of differential operating subsidies for twenty-eight shipping lines. The deadline was July 1, 1937. Kennedy was not given the job of starting the Maritime Commission's work until April 16. That gave him 75 days to finish an assignment that most shipping authorities felt could not be completed in a year. At the same time, he had to do an investigation of the whole national maritime situation in general for a comprehensive report on what was wrong with the merchant marine and what could be done to improve it, and he had to get the Maritime Commission itself functioning as an efficient and well-staffed organization.

Kennedy summoned to Washington his devoted aide, Eddie Moore, who had been working with him since his days at Hayden Stone, and two other Bostonians who had toiled with him on the SEC job, the late, brilliant John Burns, who had given up a judgeship in Massachusetts to figure out the legal aspects of the stock exchange regulations, and Joe Sheehan, whom he had known since Boston Latin School and Harvard. The three men took up bachelor quarters with Kennedy at a vast country estate that he rented at Rockville, Maryland, a luxurious place with a swimming pool where Kennedy took a long swim every morning before going to work at an early hour. They worked hard in the office for long hours during the sweltering heat of those pre-air conditioned days and carried work back to Rockville at night. Before going to bed, they sat on the terrace, listening to the symphonic recordings that Kennedy loves. Sheehan remembers one night when he and Moore, tiring of the steady classical music diet, pleaded with Kennedy for a little jazz. "You dumb bastards don't appreciate culture," Kennedy said, turning on another symphony.

Kennedy astonished the White House and the shipping

companies by completing the complicated subsidy negotiations a few days after the July 1 deadline. Then he moved on without a let-up to finish the rest of his assignment, putting the Maritime Commission into running order and delivering the overall survey of the merchant marine, in a total of ten months. "This is the toughest job I ever handled in my life, without any reservations whatever," he said when he turned in the 40,000-word survey. *Time* magazine said of the Kennedy report on U.S. shipping, "a more hard-boiled document has never come out of official Washington." Kennedy himself was hard-boiled and outspoken in his dealings with the shipping interests, the maritime unions and with Secretary of Labor Frances Perkins. At one point he declared that his opinion of the merchant marine was so low that he would never allow another one of his children to book a passage to Europe on an American-owned ship. He infuriated the labor officials by recommending that the training of seamen should be handled by the U.S. Coast Guard. Speaking to a crowd of striking longshoremen in Seattle, he said, to wild applause, "I don't know where the hell we're going to finish if we keep on the way we are going. Everybody knows the shipping business is lousy. The American merchant marine is in a mess today—it has to get new capital or be turned over to government ownership." In February, 1938, when Secretary Perkins appeared before a Senate committee and said that in her opinion the time was not yet ripe for special maritime labor legislation, Kennedy rushed to the same committee and declared, "If the maritime industry is not ripe for conciliation and mediation of its labor disputes, it is overripe for ruin." The chairman of the committee, Senator Royal Copeland, a physician, said to him, "As chairman of this committee I welcome your fury, Joe, but as a doctor I must tell you it isn't doing your stomach ulcer any good."

When Kennedy gave up his Maritime Commission chairmanship post, Roosevelt wrote to him, "Dear Joe: You have maintained your justly earned reputation of being a two-fisted, hard-hitting executive." Commenting on the relationship between the President and Kennedy during his SEC and Maritime Commission days, one Washington correspondent wrote, "Kennedy seldom goes to the President's office but he is a frequent after dinner visitor at the White House. He has a faculty for expressing opinions in short and easily understood words, not hampered by the aware-

ness that he is addressing the President of the United States."
Or, as Arthur Krock of the *New York Times* put it, "One
reason he sees the President so often is because Mr. Roosevelt
likes him as much as he respects and admires him. Pursued
by bores, the President enjoys getting away from them and
into good company."

Kennedy was still at work on the Maritime Commission
when Roosevelt offered him the ambassadorship to Great
Britain, which had been left vacant by the death of Robert
Worth Bingham. With Hitler growing stronger and more
threatening and with war clouds forming over Europe, it
was, of course, a crucial diplomatic post. When word got
out that Roosevelt was considering Kennedy for it, there
was almost as much consternation among the career men
in the State Department as there had been among the New
Deal reformers when Joe was named to the chairmanship
of the SEC. An Irish Catholic hardly seemed quite right for
the Court of St. James, especially such a hot-tempered,
blunt and outspoken one. But Roosevelt was still deeply
concerned in 1938 with economic recovery and he wanted
an ambassador in London, with Kennedy's knowledge of
finance, who could work on Anglo-American trade agreements and do something about England's war debts. And
despite Kennedy's quick tongue and flaring temper, he had
shown, in his dealings with Wall Streeters and with shipping
companies, a remarkable talent for bringing mutually suspi-
cious people to terms at a bargaining table.

After he picked Kennedy for the London assignment,
Roosevelt arranged a meeting at the White House with
him and the dignified Secretary of State Cordell Hull, so
that Hull could have a close look for the first time at the
fellow who was going to represent the United States at the
Court of St. James. Kennedy later gave a friend an entertaining account of the meeting. When he sat down with the
Roosevelt and Hull, Kennedy mentioned to the President a
luncheon conversation he had had a few days previously with
Arthur Krock. Roosevelt had recently appointed Hugo
Black to the Supreme Court. The appointment had been
followed by the sensational disclosure that Black, in his
younger days back in Alabama, had belonged to the Ku
Klux Klan. Discussing the news with Kennedy, Krock said
he was shocked that Black had accepted a seat on the Supreme Court without letting Roosevelt know about his Klan
membership. When Kennedy passed Krock's reaction on

to the President during the meeting with Hull, Roosevelt leaned back in his chair, looked at Kennedy, and said, "Joe, when Krock said that, what did you say to Krock?"

"I said to him," Kennedy replied, "if Marlene Dietrich asked you to make love to her, would you tell her you weren't much good at making love?"

Roosevelt collapsed in laughter. Cordell Hull's jaw fell open in silent amazement. Kennedy remarked afterwards, "Hull must have been saying to himself, 'My God, is this the kind of a guy we're going to send to the Court of St. James?'"

5

KENNEDY FOR PRESIDENT?

THE colorful new American Ambassador and his pretty wife and nine attractive children took London by storm. British newspapers played up the family as if they were the most fabulous Yanks to come across the Atlantic since Lindbergh, hailing the Ambassador as "Jolly Joe," "The U.S.A.'s Nine-Child Envoy" and "The Father of America," snapping pictures of him taking his morning horseback ride on Rotten Row, quoting with delight his comment that he not only understood rugby but that his oldest son, Joe, Junior, had just received a black eye playing the British football game back at Harvard. Fleet Street reporters were enchanted by Kennedy's habit of putting his feet on his desk during a press conference. Several newspapers observed humorously that the massive, thirty-six-room residence of the American Ambassador at 14 Prince's Gate, donated to the U.S. government some years before by J. P. Morgan, would be just barely big enough to accommodate the Kennedys, and all of London rocked with merriment when the owner of an apartment building being erected next door to the Prince's Gate mansion put up a sign that said, "Large Family Flats." To top it all, the Ambassador, playing his first round of golf in England a few days after his arrival, shot a hole in one. "He has made a great beginning!" the London *Daily Express* cheered. Kennedy's own statement on his achievement, a 128 yards iron shot on the Stokes Pogies course in Buckinghamshire, was rushed into print all over the British Isles: "I am much happier being the father of nine children and making a hole in one than I would be as the father of one child making a hole in nine."

The warm reception given to the Kennedys in London also brought them wide and copious publicity back in the United States. The *Ladies Home Journal* told its readers how Mrs. Kennedy maintained a card index file to keep track of the contagious diseases, inoculations, vaccinations, dental treatments, allergies and tonsilectomies of her various children, and how she dressed them all in bathing suits and bathing caps of the same color so that they could be counted more easily at the beach. The *Journal* also noted that the Kennedys had twenty-three house servants and three chauffeurs in London, with an additional force of twenty in help being hired on evenings when they were giving large dinner parties. *Time* confided that Kennedy had told Queen Elizabeth to her face that she was a cute trick, and that the Queen had been "pleased and flattered beyond words." *Colliers* said that as the purchasing agent for five girls Rose Kennedy often bought as many as two hundred dresses a year, that Joe had been doubtful about accepting the ambassadorship until somebody pointed out to him that it would make him the most important American in Europe, and that he worked in his office at the Embassy at 1 Grosvenor Square from 8:45 in the morning until 6 or 6:30 at night. When Kennedy remarked to a group of London tailors that, in his opinion, British trousers and socks were too high and British shirt tails were too long, it was boxed on the front pages of hundreds of newspapers.

There was a great to-do in the American press about the Ambassador's decision to wear long pants instead of the customary knee breeches and silk stockings when he presented himself for the first time at Buckingham Palace. In the opinion of the average U.S. newspaper editor of the Twenties and Thirties, there was enormous public interest in the length of each new envoy's pants when he turned out for his first formal appearance before the British monarchs. It was implied that a diplomat, who observed the English form of wearing knee breeches, was kowtowing too obsequiously to his hosts. Kennedy wore long pants, like Charles G. Dawes and unlike his predecessors, Andrew Mellon and Robert Worth Bingham, who followed the prescribed custom, because he was apprehensive about the cartoons and photographs of him in short pants that would surely fill the newspapers back home. It was noted that Kennedy and four of the waiters were the only men at the palace reception in full length trousers and the Queen Mother Mary was said to be rather chilly about his attire. When the Ambassador returned home for Young Joe's Harvard commencement exercises the following June, he found ship reporters in New York still asking him about the pants. Kennedy singled out one attractive girl journalist in the group and offered to prove to her in private that he had not avoided knee breeches and silk stockings because he was bow-legged.

The newspaper also made quite a bit out of the Ambassador's more serious decision to do away with the custom of presenting the daughters of socially ambitious American families at court in London. The ceremony of introducing girls from home to the Queen for no reason at all was getting out of hand and taking up too much of the Embassy's time. Kennedy put a stop to it, announcing that he would present only the daughters of American families living in England or stationed there on government assignment—a move that was warmly applauded in the States.

The younger Kennedy children, Bobby, Jean and Teddy, went to school in London. Eunice and Pat transferred from the Sacred Heart convent school in Noroton, Connecticut, to the Sacred Heart convent school in Roehampton, England, and Rosemary and Kathleen, now nineteen and seventeen, helped with the heavy social duties of the Embassy. When the family moved to England, only Young Joe and Jack stayed behind. They were both undergraduates at Harvard by then. Young Joe had studied under Harold Laski, the socialist-minded political economist, at the London School of Economics before entering college with the Class of 1938. He had decided firmly to make politics his career and his father felt that exposure to Laski's views and to the different viewpoints of the school's students, who came from all parts of the world, would be a broadening experience for him. Laski, in turn, was enchanted by Young Joe's dogged, confident and unconcealed determination to become, some day, the President of the United States. Jack also studied under Laski in London. Leaving Choate School, where he was selected as the member of his class most likely to succeed, he entered Princeton in the fall of 1935, mainly because his intimate companion at Choate, Lemoyne Billings of Baltimore, was going there. Jack had to withdraw from Princeton after a few weeks because of illness. When he recovered, he had missed too much work to catch up with his class. At his father's suggestion, he went to London and took courses with Laski for the rest of that scholastic year and the following September enrolled as a freshman at Harvard with the Class of 1940.

A sociologist or a psychiatrist might make something out of a study of the friends that the three older Kennedy boys sought at Harvard. Young Joe, Jack and Bobby, middle-class Boston Irish Catholics by birth and heritage, grew up away from Boston in a wealthy, non-Irish and Protestant atmosphere and went to rich, socially elite and non-Catholic prep schools. But at Harvard, Young Joe's inseparable companion was Ted Reardon, a Boston Irish Catholic who had to work his way through college. Jack's room mate and closest friend, Torbert Macdonald, was a Boston Irish Catholic from a family of modest means. Kenny O'Donnell, Bobby's room mate and closest friend in college, was an Irish Catholic who came from Worcester, Massachusetts, because his Bostonian father, Cleo O'Donnell, had been the football coach at Holy Cross, but a Worcester Irish Catholic and a Boston Irish Catholic are socially the same thing. Selecting such friends at Harvard instead of continuing an association with the upper crust types in their own wealthy economic level whom they had known in prep school, the Kennedys made an interesting reaching grasp at the racial, social and religious family roots from which they had been removed as children. You can take the boy out of Irish Boston but apparently it is difficult to take the Irish Boston out of the boy.

"Joe's idea of a real big evening when we were at Harvard," Ted Reardon said recently, "was to get me to bring him to my family's house in Somerville, which was not fancy, I can assure you, so that he could sit in our kitchen and eat bacon and eggs and fried potatoes that my father cooked for him. Joe thought that was really living. I couldn't quite understand it myself—here was the son of the Ambassador to Great Britain, a millionaire in his own right, who could have been at the Ritz Carlton or at Locke-Ober's in Boston, and yet all he wanted was my father to cook eggs for him in our kitchen."

Not only did all of the Kennedys pick Irish Catholic friends at Harvard; each of them became acquainted with his friend in exactly the same way. A short while ago in Washington, where he has served as Jack's administrative assistant for the past thirteen years, Reardon was asked how he met Young Joe. "We were both out for freshman football," Reardon said. "Joe was trying to make end and he was worried about his pass receiving. He asked me to stay after practice and throw passes to him." Torbert Macdonald, now a Congressman from Massachusetts, says he met Jack at freshman football practice, too. Despite his lack of weight, Jack was out for end and he also asked Macdonald, the backfield star and later the varsity captain, to toss passes to him after practice. Like Macdonald, O'Donnell was the outstanding football star in his class. Bobby, a candidate for end, came to him when they were both freshmen and asked his help in practicing pass receiving. Still devoted to Bobby, O'Donnell has worked with him in recent years on Jack's election campaigns and served as his assistant in the McClellan committee investigations.

All of the Kennedy brothers, Teddy included, were obsessed at Harvard by a burning ambition to become first-string varsity football players. Only Bobby, constructed like a rock despite his 160 pounds, was able to make it. Young Joe was on the varsity squad for three years but never made his letter against Yale. The skinny and fragile Jack was dropped to the junior varsity as a sophomore. Scrimmaging in practice against the much heavier varsity team, Jack received the serious spinal injury that was to plague him for the next fifteen years. In his college days the Ambassador never attempted to play football but, just like Jack and Bobby, his close friend at Harvard was the gridiron star of his class, Bob Fisher.

Young Joe and Jack were busily engaged in undergraduate life at Harvard. Joe played rugby, which was then being introduced as a springtime sport in the Ivy League, served on the student council for three years and was its chairman as a senior, belonged to the Hasty Pudding and Pi Eta and, although too carefree to be a really deep student, he was graduated *cum laude*. Jack majored in government under Professor Arthur Holcombe, who taught all the Kennedy boys and who regards Jack as an outstanding intellectual. Professor Holcombe found that, even as a youngster at Harvard, Jack had a profound and lively interest in the science of politics. He wrote a notable paper under the professor's guidance, on the career of an obscure politician in New York State, which analyzed the mistakes that had kept the frustrated office seeker from gaining prominence. But at that time Jack was reluctant to consider politics as a career for himself. Young Joe had already staked a claim on the presidency and one politician seemed to be enough in the family. Besides, as interested as he was in political theory and the problems of government, he shied away from handshaking and back-slapping requirements of the vote getter, at which Young Joe excelled. Along with his studies, Jack worked on the editorial staff of the *Harvard Crimson*, played on his Winthrop House hockey team and did well on the swimming team until his disastrous attempt to qualify for the Yale meet while confined to a sick bed with a fever in the Stillman Infirmary.

When the Ambassador came to Cambridge for Young Joe's graduation in June, 1938, his sons noticed that a chill had developed in their father's relationship with Roosevelt. Bargaining with the British on reciprocal trade agreements and on resumption of war debt payments, the main assignments the President had given to Kennedy when he sent him to London, had gone badly. With Hitler about to march on Czechoslovakia, the British were too preoccupied with European unrest to be bothered with trade and old debts from the last war. The Ambassador replied tersely to questioning reporters at the Harvard commencement that it was a poor time to reach trade agreements. "The war debt question is not before me," he added, closing the interview. There were other reasons for Roosevelt's coolness. Several Washington correspondents reported to their editors that Kennedy had been sending letters from London to certain columnists and reporters in the capital containing information about the trade and debt negotiations which had not reached the State Department or the White House. Some of these letters, it was said, had been turned over to Roosevelt.

And there was growing talk that Kennedy would be a Democratic candidate for President in 1940. He was in an enviable position with his creditable performances in the SEC and Maritime Commission jobs, the acclaim he had been receiving for getting along so well with the British, and, more important, his unique status as one of the very few New Deal Democrats who was looked upon favorably by big business. Kennedy's publicity had been magnificent. He was getting high praise from the Henry Luce publications, *Time* and *Life*, and when he came from London for Young Joe's commencement, his warm admirer, Arthur Krock, wrote in *The New York Times*, "Well, here is Mr. Kennedy back again, the rage of London, the best copy in the British (and Irish) press, his counsel steadily sought by the statesmen, his influence manifest and powerful in all matters in which the United States has an interest in Great Britain. He is back, undazzled by such a taking-up socially and officially as no American perhaps has known abroad since Franklin's day."

In the opinion of political observers at the time, Kennedy's out-of-channels correspondence with Washington newspapermen seemed to tie in with the talk of his running for

President; it looked as if he was handing out inside news about his work in London to keep his name alive back home. Roosevelt may have thought so, too. From Harvard, the Ambassador went to Hyde Park to have a long talk with the President. The anti-Roosevelt *Chicago Tribune*, quoting the usual unimpeachable sources, said that the conversation "was carried on in a frigid atmosphere because Mr. Roosevelt has received positive evidence that Kennedy hopes to use the Court of St. James as a stepping stone to the White House in 1940."

If Roosevelt was chilly toward Kennedy in that June of 1938, he must have felt colder during and after the Munich crisis a few months later. In London, Kennedy had become a close and constantly consulted friend of Tory Prime Minister Neville Chamberlain, the umbrella man, and Chamberlain's fellow appeasers in the government, Sir Horace Wilson and Sir John Simon. Like them, Kennedy felt that their backing-down to Hitler in the Czechoslovakian dispute had insured peace in our time. He almost said as much publicly that October in a speech at the Trafalgar Day Dinner of the British Navy League.

The Ambassador began his talk to the Navy League by remarking that his wife had gotten nervous when she found out what he was planning to say. "Have you thought how this would sound back home?" he quoted Rose as saying. "You don't want folks to get the idea that you are seeing things through English eyes." In effect, Kennedy said that the world was big enough for both the democracies and the dictatorships, and there was no reason why they couldn't get along together without war:

"It has long been a theory of mine that it is unproductive for both the democratic and dictator countries to widen the division now existing between them by emphasizing their differences, which are now self-apparent. Instead of hammering away at what are regarded as irreconcilables, they could advantageously bend their energies toward solving their common problems by an attempt to re-establish good relations on a world basis.

"It is true that the democratic and dictator countries have important and fundamental divergencies of outlook, which in certain matters go deeper than politics. But there is simply no sense, common or otherwise, in letting these differences grow into unrelenting antagonisms. After all, we have to live together in the same world, whether we like it or not."

Roosevelt, to be sure, had not yet taken an open stand against the Munich agreement but Kennedy's words must have been hard for the President to swallow. It was also hard for Winston Churchill, Sir Anthony Eden and other members of the Opposition in England to swallow, and they regarded it as interference in Britain's own affairs.

A month later the Ambassador was in the news again with a plan to remove Germany's 600,000 Nazi-persecuted Jews from their homeland and resettle them in British colonies and various other sparsely populated parts of the world. This proposal was hailed in the next week's issue of *Life*. "Kennedy is rated the most influential U.S. Ambassador to England in many years," *Life* said. "If his plan for settling the German Jews, already widely known as the 'Kennedy Plan,' succeeds, it will add new luster to a reputation which may well carry Joseph Patrick Kennedy into the White House."

In Washington, however, both Secretary of State Hull and Roosevelt told newsmen that they knew nothing about the widely known Kennedy Plan. "Hull came as near to being tart as he ever does in his comments on Kennedy's reported activities," one correspondent wrote. Indirectly, the Administration handed the Kennedy Plan and Kennedy a rebuke by announcing later that Myron C. Taylor was to be the United States' spokesman on all questions concerning European refugees.

In December, when Kennedy was coming home to spend Christmas as usual at Palm Beach with his family, one Washington correspondent close to Roosevelt, Kenneth Crawford of the *New York Post*, wrote an inside dope dispatch which said that the Ambassador would be hauled over the coals by the President and by the State Department for the Navy League speech and the Kennedy Plan and for a report from London that he had used his influence to censor from a Paramount movie newsreel, before it was shown in England, critical comments by two British newspaper editors about Chamberlain's foreign policy. "Leaders of the opposition to Prime Minister Chamberlain within Great Britain feel that Kennedy has allowed his friendship for the Tories to lead him into improper activities and have conveyed their complaints directly to the President," Crawford wrote.

While he was in Palm Beach, Kennedy made the news

section of *Life* again with another item that must have annoyed Roosevelt no end. A caption under a picture of the Ambassador smiling in the Florida sun mentioned that he had divulged to Walter Winchell that during the Munich crisis he had persuaded Colonel Charles A. Lindbergh to give the famous Lindbergh estimate of the impressive strength of German air power to Chamberlain. It was intimated that Lindbergh's awesome respect for what Hitler could do from the air may have been a factor in Chamberlain's appeasement move.

Until that Christmas of 1938, Kennedy had been, like Neville Chamberlain, fairly optimistic about the chances of averting war in Europe. When he returned to London in January, he changed his opinion and began to send Washington repeated warnings that war would break out before 1939 was over. At that time Jack, a junior at Harvard, had accumulated enough credits after the mid-term examinations to take the rest of the college year off from classes. He went to Europe and spent six months there, working for his father in London and for Ambassador William C. Bullitt in the American Embassy in Paris, and traveling in Germany and eastern Europe. Young Joe was also seeing Europe, touring civil-war torn Spain and making a trip to Russia. He went abroad for a year after he was graduated from Harvard, returning to Cambridge in the fall of 1939 to enter Harvard Law School. That August the two boys joined the rest of the family for a few weeks of vacation near Cannes on the Riviera. Toward the end of the month, Jack went to Germany and the other Kennedys traveled back to London with their father and mother. The night that Jack was leaving Berlin, the U.S. Charge d'Affairs, Alex Kirk, gave him a message to bring to his father: there would be war within one week. There was.

At three o'clock in the morning, the day after war was declared, the Ambassador was awakened in the country house to which he had hurriedly moved his family from London. He was told that the British liner *Athenia* was sinking in the North Atlantic, torpedoed by a German submarine, with 1,418 people aboard, 300 of them Americans. The Ambassador woke up Jack and immediately sent him to Glasgow with Eddie Moore to take care of American survivors who were being brought to Scotland and, equally important, to find out from them how the disaster had happened. The Germans were already saying officially that the

British had sunk the ship themselves to arouse American sympathy.

It was an uncomfortable and trying assignment for a twenty-one-year-old college undergraduate. Just that week, back in Washington, the President, trying to avoid any sort of show of American arms abroad that might be mistaken for a violation of neutrality, had ruled that U.S. Navy vessels could not be used to convoy war refugees in European waters. The American survivors from the *Athenia* who confronted Jack in Glasgow did not want to attempt another trip home on the Atlantic on the American ship *Orizaba* that was being sent for them, unless they had Navy protection. Jack had to tell them they could not have a convoy. After twelve hours in life boats at sea, they were in no mood to listen to his arguments. "We've got six billion dollars worth of United States Navy and they won't do this for us?" one angry man from New Jersey yelled at him. Jack tried persuasion, pointing out that they would be safer on an American ship without a convoy than on a British vessel guarded by a whole fleet. A college girl shook her fist at him and said the survivors would refuse to go home. Jack was glad to leave Glasgow with his detailed report on the sinking, which left no doubt that the *Athenia* had been fired upon without warning by an enemy submarine. Many of the third class passengers, Jack found out, had been trapped and drowned below decks.

Joe Kennedy responded to the strain of heavy work and responsibility thrown upon his Embassy by the outbreak of the war with snap and efficiency. There were some nine thousand Americans in England for him to keep an eye on, British government officials to be seen and Secretary of State Hull and President Roosevelt to be kept informed by transatlantic telephone and priority cables. *Time* magazine described him, in that first hectic week in September, in shirt sleeves at his desk, grabbing by turns at three phones, "tugging at his black suspenders, cussing, grumbling incoherently, snapping popgun orders." That fall, as the war settled into its early and deceptive "phony" stage, with German soldiers opposite the untouched Maginot Line displaying signs to the French which said, "We have orders not to fire on you until you fire on us," Kennedy made a trip to Washington to report to Roosevelt. Impressed by Germany's military power and discouraged by Britain's woeful lack of armaments and France's internal confusion

nd panic, he felt, as did Ambassador Bullitt at the time, that
he Allies had no chance of victory. Kennedy told Roosevelt
hat sending aid to Britain would only be throwing it down
he drain. He said the same thing to newspaper reporters
nd quoted odds to them against the Allies, perhaps not
ealizing that his comments would appear in British, as well
s American, papers. When he returned to London, he found
o his hurt dismay that he had lost his popularity in England.
The British had come to think of him as one of their own,"
ne American correspondent wrote from London. "They
xpected him to plead the British cause when he went home.
oe was shocked by the changed atmosphere. He spent more
ime with Embassy people and American friends since the
British social invitations were not as numerous as in pre-war
imes." He was also lonely because his wife and children
ad been sent back to Bronxville when the war started.
Kathleen had taken a job as a reporter with the *Washington
Times Herald*. Young Joe was at Harvard Law School. Jack,
t Harvard as a senior, was writing a thesis about the un-
ealistic lack of preparedness for war that he had seen in
England. Arthur Krock later urged him to expand it into
a book, *Why England Slept*, which was published in 1940
with a warmly approving preface by Henry Luce, who said
hat he hoped it would be read by one million Americans.
Highly praised by reviewers and coming out at a time when
he danger of war was on everybody's mind, it was an
mmediate best seller, 55,000 copies in the United States and
5,000 in England. Jack gave all of his British royalties from
he book to the bombed town of Plymouth. With the Amer-
can royalties he bought himself a Buick.

The following year, 1940, the year of the fall of France,
Dunkirk and the Battle of Britain, was a miserable year for
he Ambassador. With F.D.R. running again, there was no
White House hope for Joe Kennedy. In his position in
ombed London, he felt hopeless and frustrated. He asked
o be relieved; knowing that the United States was arming,
e felt that he would be more useful and more important in
key defense production post in Washington. He had ur-
ently advised Roosevelt that in backing England to the hilt
he President would be "left holding the bag in a war in
which the Allies expect to be beaten." But Roosevelt had
gnored Kennedy and had made the momentous decision,
n the face of the coming 1940 election, of standing behind
he British to the end. Kennedy's pessimism was understand-

able and logical. That June, after the evacuation of Dunkirk, Winston Churchill delivered his memorable radio address which ended with the words, "We shall fight on the beaches, we shall fight on the landing grounds, we shall fight in the fields and in the streets." Then Churchill covered the microphone with his hand, turned with a smile to the Dean of Canterbury who was sitting beside him and muttered, "And we will hit them over the heads with beer bottles, which is all we have really got." As a matter of fact, the British actually were preparing to fight off the expected invasion of Hitler with beer bottles containing sulphur and TNT.

Outwardly, Kennedy appeared to get along well with Churchill after he succeeded Chamberlain as prime minister, but Churchill never forgot Kennedy's support of the Tory appeasers. When Harry Hopkins visited Churchill in 1941, he wrote to Roosevelt, "I told him there was a feeling in some quarters that he, Churchill, did not like America, Americans or Roosevelt. This set him off on a bitter tho fairly constrained attack on Ambassador Kennedy, who he believes is responsible for this impression." The big question about Kennedy in Washington during that summer of 1940 was why Roosevelt continued to keep an ambassador in London who so strenuously opposed the Administration's pro-British policy, especially in view of Kennedy's repeated requests to be relieved. There was agreement with a theory outlined by Joseph Alsop and Robert Kintner in their newspaper column, which they described as highly vouched-for: "The President regards Kennedy as likely to do less harm in London than in New York," Alsop and Kintner wrote. "An emotional fellow, he has strong convictions. He will certainly express his opinions to every available American listener the instant he gets through the customs. He will be in a position to speak impressively and persuasively. The President is represented as fearing he will reduce large numbers of leaders of opinion to such a state of hopeless blue funk that our foreign policy will be half-immobilized by fear. In short, the President has repeatedly urged Kennedy to remain in London in order to keep him quiet."

But in October, Kennedy packed up to go back to the United States to speak on Roosevelt's behalf in his bid for a third term, and, although there was no announcement of his retirement from the ambassadorship, Joe let it be known privately that he probably would not be returning to London. The British gave him a warm sendoff. He was photographed shaking hands with Winston Churchill at 10 Downing Street. The King and Queen invited him to a Sunday luncheon and he came back later that same afternoon to have tea with Their Majesties and Princess Elizabeth and Princess Margaret. As a souvenir of wartime London, Joe took home with him an air raid siren, which he said he would use at Hyannis Port to call the children from their boats at dinner time. The *Evening News* noted that the Air Ministry had renamed its Douglas DB7 bombers "The Bostons" as a tribute to Kennedy's birthplace, and said, "It is Mr. Kennedy singlehanded who has strengthened Anglo-American friendship in London." The *Daily Herald* devoted one of Hannen Swaffer's widely-read columns to Kennedy, quoting him as saying respectfully about the bombing of London, "I did not know London could take it. I did not think any city could take it. I am bowed in reverence." Swaffer gave Kennedy credit for proposing the highly successful 1939 visit of the King and Queen to the United States, and concluded his column with: "Forever, in deeds if not in written words, Britain and America are Allies. Largely, that is Joseph Kennedy's work. Goodbye, Joe! Heaven bless you! Your job is done."

Apparently Joe did not feel that the job was quite done because as soon as he landed in New York he invited newspapers and wire services to send reporters to a press conference at the Waldorf Astoria. As Alsop and Kintner had predicted, he was ready to express opinions as soon as he passed through customs. One of the reporters who rushed to the Waldorf Astoria that day remembers that Kennedy never appeared and that after a long delay a spokesman informed the gathering that the press conference had been cancelled. Apparently, Roosevelt had gotten to Kennedy before he talked.

A few days later, October 29, the returned Ambassador delivered a radio speech backing Roosevelt for President that the editors of *Life* described later as probably the most effective vote-getting speech of the 1940 campaign. "More than anything else it allayed fear that Mr. Roosevelt would 'take this country into war,'" *Life* said. The Kennedy talk urged aid to England but advocated a stern and relentless refrain from military entanglement in the European war. It was what most Americans wanted to hear, and coming from Roosevelt's own Ambassador to Great Britain, it made Roosevelt look good.

During the following week, Kennedy was in Boston, visiting Joe and Jack at Harvard, and stopping at the Ritz Carlton. Louis Lyons of the *Boston Globe* visited him at the hotel with Ralph Coglan of the *St. Louis Post Dispatch* and Charles Edmondson, another *Post Dispatch* man, who was studying at Harvard on a Nieman journalism fellowship. The visit seemed to Kennedy to be informal—he was eating apple pie and cheese with his suspenders hanging from his hips when the newspapermen dropped in—and, as he said afterwards, he assumed that anything he said would be off the record. Lyons did not understand it that way.

Kennedy told his visitors that he was in favor of all-out economic aid to England, but no military aid, in order to give America time to arm itself. "I'm willing to spend all I've got to keep us out of the war," Lyons quoted him as saying. "There's no sense in our getting in. We'd only be holding the bag. What would we get out of it? Democracy is finished in England. It isn't that she's fighting for democracy. That's the bunk. She's fighting for self-preservation, just as we will if it comes to us. As long as she can hold out, give her what it takes, whatever we don't have to have, and don't expect anything back."

Mentioning Roosevelt's leading critic, the isolationist Charles A. Lindbergh, Kennedy said, "Lindbergh isn't crazy either, you know." He also had some things to say about Eleanor Roosevelt: "She bothered us more on our jobs in Washington to take care of the poor little nobodies than all the rest of the people down there put together. She's always sending me a note to have some little Susie Glotz to tea at the Embassy."

If Roosevelt had any intention of sending Kennedy back to London or if Kennedy had any hope of continuing in a high position in government, both notions were dispelled when Lyons' full and direct quotation of the interview appeared in the next morning's *Boston Globe*, and in most of the other newspapers in the country and abroad. Kennedy's remarks, especially the one about democracy being finished in England, created a storm. The New York *Herald Tribune* said editorially, "If Mr. Kennedy is not an out-and-out advocate of appeasement, he is nevertheless a defeatist of the first order." Kennedy could only say that he was under the impression that the interview was off the record and that the published story "creates a different impression entirely than I would want to set forth." He quickly offered his resignation as Ambassador to the Court of St. James, and, just as quickly, it was accepted.

6

A MESSAGE ON A COCONUT

THE summer of 1940 was the last time that all
of the nine Kennedy children were together at Hyannis
Port and it was a happy, busy and exciting summer that none
of them would forget. The older ones were now grown up,
glamorous figures in the eyes of their dazzled younger
brothers and sisters, well-traveled, with fabulous experiences
in college and in Europe, involved in big accomplishments,
filled with great plans and great talk. Young Joe was already
a politician. That summer he had been a Massachusetts delegate to the Democratic national convention, and a controversial one, too. Pledged to James A. Farley's candidacy like
the rest of the state delegation, he had stubbornly refused to
switch his vote when the party leaders wanted to re-nominate
Roosevelt by unanimous acclaim. Jack was the author of a
best-selling book. Kathleen was a newspaperwoman on the
Washington *Times Herald*. But at Hyannis Port they still
threw themselves eagerly and loudly into the family touch
football games on the front lawn, paired off in grim, slam-
bang mixed doubles tennis matches on the court behind the
house, that usually ended with one of the girls in tears, sailed
in inter-club races against boats from Wianno and Osterville,
organized trips to Turner's on Route 28 for ice cream, and,
every evening after dinner, they still gathered with neighbors
downstairs in the family's private projection room to watch
a new first-run movie that the Ambassador's former associates
in the film industry provided for their pleasure.

The large Kennedy house and its long porch was so filled
that summer with college and school friends and so noisy
with clashing conversation and horse play that Rose Kennedy
often slipped away and hid herself in her small cabana at
the edge of the lawn near the beach to get a few hours of
peace. One week end, Charles Spaulding, now one of Jack's
closest friends, was brought to the Kennedy place by a Yale
classmate whom he was visiting on Cape Cod. Spaulding has
a vivid remembrance of his first look at the Kennedys. "I

was fascinated by them," Spaulding says. "Jack was auto-
graphing copies of *Why England Slept* while Grandfather
Fitzgerald was reading to him a political story from a newspaper. Young Joe was telling about something that happened
to him in Russia. Mrs. Kennedy was talking on the phone
with Cardinal Spellman. A tall and very attractive girl in a
sweat shirt and dungarees, who turned out to be Pat, was
describing how a German Messerschmitt plane had crashed
near her father's house outside of London. Bobby was trying
to get everybody to play charades. The next thing I knew
all of us were choosing up sides for touch football, and
Kathleen was calling the plays in the huddle for the team
I was on. There was something doing every minute. The
conversation at the dinner table was wonderful, lively and
entertaining, ranging from the war and Washington politics
to books, sports and show business. I don't think America
has ever had another family quite like the Kennedys—inde-
pendently wealthy, and yet so realistic, unaffected and down
to earth and so deeply and seriously concerned with what's
going on in the world and so anxious to work hard in public
service."

Spaulding, a thoughtful and well-read fellow, believes that
the Kennedys are a throwback to the colorful Whig landed
gentry of eighteenth and early nineteenth century England
that are described in David Cecil's biography of William
Lamb, *The Young Melbourne*. Cecil does indeed sound as if
he is talking about the Kennedys when he draws a picture
of a typical family of sporty, democratic Whig aristocrats:
"The Whig lord was so often as not a minister, his eldest
son an M.P., his second attached to a foreign embassy, so
that their houses were alive with the effort and hurry of
politics. Red Foreign office boxes strewed the library tables;
at any time of day or night a courier might come galloping
up with critical news, and the minister must post off to
London to attend a Cabinet meeting. Whig society itself
was a sort of club, exclusive, but in which those who managed to achieve membership lived on equal terms; a rowdy,
rough-and-tumble club, full of conflict and plain speaking,
where people were expected to stand up for themselves and
give and take hard knocks. . . Born and bred citizens of the
world, they knew their way about it by a sort of infallible
instinct. And they had an instinctive mastery of its social
arts. Their negligence was never boorish; it arose from the
fact that they felt so much at home in life that they were

careless of its conventions. Superficial brusqueness masked an unfailing adroitness in the management of situations; their talk was as dexterous as it was unaffected; its bluntness was made delightful by their peculiar brand of jovial incisive humor. For they possessed—it was their chief charm—in the highest degree, the high spirits of their home."

Like the Whigs, and like the Proper Bostonians that the Ambassador resented in his younger days, the Kennedys grew up with a strong respect for their own family. Paul Dever, the late governor of Massachusetts, may have been thinking as much of their family pride as he was of their wealth and social standing when he said that the Kennedys were the first Irish Brahmins. Approval within the family means more to them, their friends say, than outside acclaim. "Most youngsters, as they grow up, seek their main stimulation and interests outside the home but the Kennedys found these things in their own family circle," says their friend, Justice William O. Douglas of the Supreme Court. "After all, it was an exciting home, a good place to be, full of fun and games and plenty of fascinating talk about world affairs and world leaders. It was hard for them to find anything as attractive outside. This is why they are so attached to each other, and so secure." Such insular security has also made them self centered; one of the Kennedy girls has said that it seemed for awhile as if none of them would ever get interested enough in anybody outside of the family to get married. Harold H. Martin wrote about the Kennedys in the *Saturday Evening Post*: "When an outsider threatens to thwart the ambitions of any of them, the whole family forms a close-packed ring, horns lowered, like a herd of bison beset by wolves."

After he resigned as Ambassador, Joe Kennedy kept on speaking up loudly against American involvement in the war right up until the attack on Pearl Harbor. On January 18, 1941, he made a notable and widely quoted radio speech opposing Roosevelt's policy of all-out aid to England and Lend-Lease. Kennedy said again that he, too, favored "utmost" aid to England but not beyond "the absolute minimum necessary for our own protection." "This is not our war," he said. "We were not consulted when it began. We have no veto power over its continuance. It does happen that England's spirited defense is greatly to our advantage. Therefore we ought to arm to the teeth and give as much help as we can. But let us do it on the basis of preserving American ideals and interests." That spring at Oglethorpe University in Atlanta he said, "This country must not become a belligerent just because we love Churchill and hate Hitler. We cannot divert the tides of mighty revolution now sweeping Asia and Europe. An attempt to do so would end in failure and disgrace at abroad, in disillusionment and bankruptcy at home."

Young Joe echoed his father's anti-aggression sentiments and helped to organize a stay-out-of-war group at Harvard. But in June, 1941, after finishing his second year at Harvard Law School, he joined the Navy as an aviation cadet and received his commission and wings the following May. Jack tried to get into the Navy and the Army but was turned down because of the spinal injury that he suffered playing football as a Harvard sophomore. He went through an intensive series of exercises and treatments to strengthen his back and applied again for a Navy commission. This time he was accepted and assigned to intelligence desk work in Washington, which he found suffocating. He pulled strings for a transfer to the company of Torbert Macdonald and other Harvard, Yale and Princeton friends in the more informal and dashing and strongly Ivy League atmosphere of the torpedo boat training station at Melville, Rhode Island.

One of Kennedy's comrades in the PT boat service, the red-haired Paul Fay, Jr., of San Francisco, was recalling recently how he met Jack at Melville. "The first thing I did when I landed at Melville was to dig up a football and round up a bunch of the new guys who came there with me for a game of touch," Fay said. "We started to play and this skinny kid in a Harvard football sweater came walking down to the field and watched us. He asked if he could get into the game. I said sure, if he got another guy for the other team, which he did in a few minutes. Well, he wasn't in the game five minutes before he started arguing with me about the rules. I wanted to brain him. I figured he was one of the officers' kids. Well, the next day we started classes on how to operate the boats and it turns out that this same skinny kid is our instructor."

Jack stayed at Melville until he learned that he was about to be sent to a PT squadron in the peaceful area of the Panama Canal. Again he pulled strings in the Washington office of the Secretary of the Navy, James V. Forrestal, an old friend of his father from Wall Street. Jack asked for combat duty in the Pacific and his request was granted. He went to a squadron based at the island of Rendova, south of New Georgia, where he was made the skipper of PT-109 with a crew of two other officers and ten enlisted men.

Shortly after taking over the boat, on the night of August 2, 1943, Kennedy was on patrol in Blackett Strait in the Solomon Island, forty miles from his base. It was a pitch dark night with no moon or stars in sight. Kennedy was leading three other boats in search of a Japanese target. He was at the wheel and his executive officer, a tall and husky Princeton graduate named George Ross, was on watch at the bow of the boat with binoculars. Before they saw it in time to turn away, a Japanese destroyer loomed up out of the darkness and drove into the PT boat's middle, cutting it in two. Kennedy remembers that the crash did not even slow down the speed of the fast destroyer. He was thrown against the cockpit and landed flat on his back on the deck, injuring again the spinal vertebrae that had been dislocated in the football scrimmage at Harvard. There was an explosion that lit up the destroyer and gasoline began to burn on the water.

Kennedy saw that the front half of the boat, on which he was crouching with four other men, was being kept afloat by the sealed watertight bulkheads in the bow. The other PTs in the patrol were nowhere in sight and the destroyer had disappeared. Seeing the crash, the burst of flame and the burning gasoline, the other Americans assumed that the 109 had gone down with all hands, and did not return to the scene to search for survivors.

Calling and flashing a light in the darkness, Kennedy located Ross and five of the enlisted men swimming in the water near the floating half of the wrecked boat. Two of them, a fellow Bostonian named Harris and the boat's engineer, McMahon, who was trapped below deck in the collision and badly burned, were drifting a hundred yards away. Kennedy dove into the water and swam to them, towing McMahon back to the floating hulk. A breeze blew the remainder of the boat away from them steadily and it seemed as if they would never reach it. Harris said he thought he couldn't make it. Kennedy turned to him sternly and said, "For a guy from Boston, you're certainly putting up a great exhibition out here, Harris." Counting heads when everybody had gotten to the boat, Kennedy found that eleven of the thirteen had survived. Two of the enlisted men were never seen after the collision.

The next day, while they waited in vain for rescuers, the

wrecked half of the boat turned over in the water and they saw it would soon sink. The group decided to swim to a small island three miles away. There were other islands bigger and nearer but the Navy officers knew that they were occupied by the Japanese. On one island, only one mile to the south, they could see a Japanese camp. McMahon, the engineer whose legs were disabled by burns, was unable to swim. Despite his own painfully crippled back, Kennedy swam the three miles with a breast stroke, towing behind him by a life belt strap that he held between his teeth the helpless McMahon. Every few minutes, as Kennedy recalled later, he would have to stop and rest, taking the life belt out of his mouth and holding it in his hand. He would ask the engineer, "How do you feel, Mac?" McMahon would always make the same reply: "I'm okay, Mr. Kennedy. How are you?" It took Kennedy and the suffering engineer five hours to reach the island.

There was nothing on the tiny island except a few palm trees with coconuts on them. After a short rest ashore, Kennedy decided to leave the other men and swim to Ferguson Passage on the far side of another island nearby. Boats from his PT squadron had been going through Ferguson Passage on recent nights and Kennedy was hoping to hail one of them. He took with him a heavy ship's lantern, salvaged from the crash, with which to signal. All that night he was in the water, swimming and drifting in a daze, but there were no PT boats in Ferguson Passage that night. In the morning he made his way back painfully to the rest of the survivors and collapsed from exhaustion and hunger. George Ross watched Ferguson Passage the following night but there were no PTs to be seen then, either.

On the third day after the wrecking of the boat, Kennedy decided to move the group to another island to the southeast, slightly larger, with what seemed to be more coconuts and nearer to the PT squadron's route through Ferguson Passage. The swim to the new refuge lasted for three hours, with Kennedy again pulling McMahon by holding the life belt strap between his teeth. Finding coconuts on the ground at the island, the men drank milk from them and became sick. When it rained that night, they licked rain drops from the leaves of bushes and then found that the leaves were soiled by bird dung. Disgruntled, hungry and thirsty, with nothing to drink except the coconut milk that nauseated them, and no food except a few live snails that tasted bitter, their spirits reached a new low. To distract them and give them some hope, Kennedy persuaded Ross to swim with him to Nauru Island, closer still to Ferguson Passage.

On Nauru, Kennedy and Ross stumbled on a wonderful find, a Japanese shelter with a keg of water and a box of hardtack biscuits and hard candy. Nearby they also found a dugout native canoe, big enough to hold one of them. After dark, Kennedy paddled in the canoe back to the others in the group with water and hardtack crackers. The next day he went again to Nauru in the canoe to rejoin Ross. While he was on the water, a storm came up and swamped the canoe, but he was miraculously saved from drowning by a group of Solomon Island natives who suddenly came up beside him in a large dugout canoe. The natives took him to Nauru and showed him and Ross where a two-man canoe was hidden there. Kennedy took out his jack knife and scratched a message on a smooth coconut shell: "Native knows posit he can pilot 11 alive need small boat Kennedy." He gave the coconut shell to the natives and tried to tell them to take it to Rendova. They nodded and paddled away.

That night Kennedy and Ross went out on Ferguson Passage in the two-man canoe in search of PT boats. A violent storm came up, swamping the canoe and almost drowning them. In the morning they were awakened by four natives. One of the natives said to Kennedy in an impeccable British accent, "I have a letter for you, sir." It was from a New Zealand infantry officer on New Georgia who had received word of Kennedy's whereabouts. It said, "To Senior Officer, Nauru Is. Have just learned of your presence on Nauru Is. and also that two natives have taken news to Rendova. I strongly advise you return immediately to here in this canoe and by the time you arrive I will be in radio communication with authorities at Rendova and we can finalize plans to collect balance of your party. Will warn aviation of your crossing Ferguson Passage. Lt. Wincote."

The four natives in their big canoe took Kennedy and Ross to the rest of the survivors on the smaller island and cooked for everybody, on an alcohol stove, a glorious feast of C-rations. Then Kennedy stretched out in their canoe, covered from the view of enemy planes by foliage, and made the trip to Lieutenant Wincote in New Georgia. That night he met a PT boat at a rendezvous point. Somebody aboard called to him, "Hey, Jack! We've got some food for you!"

Kennedy remembers yelling back, "No, thanks. I just had a coconut."

As was customary in such cases, the survivors were ordered to return to stateside duty after their rescue. Kennedy astonished everybody at Rendova by refusing to go. Asked about this recently, he shrugged his shoulders and said, "I had just gotten out there when this thing happened. I didn't want to turn around and go back to the States so soon." He succeeded in concealing from his commanding officers the extent of his spinal injury and asked to take over another boat and a new crew and to go back into more combat. Al Cluster of Van Nuys, California, his squadron commander, assigned him to the PT 59 which they converted from a torpedo boat to a heavily armed small gunboat with additional 50-calibre machine guns and 40-millimeter Bofors automatics. The Navy's work in the South Pacific then no longer required the high-speed hit and run torpedo missions for which the PT boats were designed; there were few Japanese big ships left in the area and most of the remaining enemy targets were supply barges that were operating close to shore. Turning the PTs into gun boats was gross miscasting and made them dangerously vulnerable. The heavy extra loading of added guns, ammunition and extra crewmen to man the guns slowed the motor boats down and made them labor in moderate weather. "With all those extra guys on it, sleeping all over the place and bulging out of the hatchways, Jack's boat looked like one of those Oakie jallopies in *The Grapes of Wrath*," says Red Fay who was with him at the time of the gunboat experiment. "He used to say to me, 'Can't I come over and eat with you tonight just to get away from all these faces that are always hanging over me?'"

"Working against Jap barges close to shore with a slow overloaded PT like that was really perilous and terribly exposed fighting, but Jack kept at it," Al Cluster says. "It got so that the crew didn't like to go out with him because he took so many chances. He even wanted to make a run up the Choiseul River, which was loaded with Japanese guns. Finally he began to realize that our experiment with the beautiful little gunboats was less than a complete success, and it was only then that we were able to persuade him to go home and get his back looked at. I'll never forget the way he insisted on staying on the job when he had a legitimate reason for returning to the States that any of us would have jumped at. This trait of devotion or obligation, or what-have-you, is, in my opinion, as important a facet of Jack as his courage. It wasn't recklessness, but a mature dedication to service not often seen by any of us."

The Kennedys were at their Palm Beach home when Jack arrived in California and obtained leave. He headed for Florida and found Chuck Spaulding with his father and mother when he ran into the house. "As soon as he dropped his bags and said hello to us, he wanted to go out right away to a night club and live it up," Spaulding recalls. "I guess when he was hanging onto that wrecked half of PT boat in the South Pacific, Jack thought he would never see a pretty girl or hear dance music ever again."

The coconut shell scratched with the message for help is now on Kennedy's desk in the Senate Office Building in Washington. Framed on the wall of the office, along with a 99-pound sailfish, 9 feet and 8 inches long, that he caught on his honeymoon at Acapulco in 1953, and the citation that he received with his honorary degree at Harvard ("Brave officer, able Senator, son of Harvard; loyal to party, he remains steadfast to principle.") is the letter from Lieutenant Wincote that was handed to him by the English-speaking native on Nauru Island. In October, 1957, the nation's television audience saw the ordeal of the survivors of PT-109 re-enacted on the Navy Log show. The Senator helped as a technical consultant in its preparation. Some of the dialogue, he said, made him feel "slightly embarrassed." (One of the actors in the show, playing the part of an enlisted man, says of Skipper Kennedy at one point, "Let me tell you, there's a guy.") When that Navy Log drama was shown on the ABC television network, one of the people who happened to miss it was Jack Kennedy. He was in Jackson, Mississippi, that night, delivering a speech to the Young Democrats.

7

YOUNG JOE AND KATHLEEN

Bob Considine, the Hearst star reporter, wrote a series of newspaper articles on the Kennedy family in 1957 which he entitled "The Amazing Kennedys." While he was gathering material for the articles, Considine, along with Bill Cunningham, the *Boston Herald* columnist, and a few other guests, had lunch with the Ambassador and Mrs. Kennedy at their Palm Beach home. During the meal, Considine asked the Ambassador to tell him about Young Joe. The father thought about his oldest son for a few moments and then broke into tears.

"It was a terrible thing to see," Considine said later. "He sat there at the table weeping, unable to speak or to control himself, for almost five minutes. It seemed to the rest of us like an hour. Finally, he pulled himself together and wiped his eyes but still he couldn't talk. He gestured toward his wife and said, 'She can tell you about him. I can't.'"

A few days later in Washington Considine asked Jack Kennedy about his dead older brother.

"Joe was the star of our family," Jack said. "He did everything better than the rest of us. If he had lived he would have gone on in politics and he would have been elected to the House and to the Senate as I was. And, like me, he would have gone for the vice-presidential nomination at the 1956 convention, but, unlike me, he wouldn't have been beaten. Joe would have won the nomination." Jack paused, smiled, and added, "And then he and Stevenson would have been beaten by Eisenhower, and today Joe's political career would be in shambles and he would be trying to pick up the pieces."

Handsome, bright and charming, Young Joe made a powerful impression on everybody who knew him. His influence upon his younger brothers was especially strong. Jack's and Bobby's hard competitive drive and enormous, untiring capacity for work come as much from imitating Young Joe as from the inspiration of their father. In *As We Remember Joe*, he wrote: "I think that if the Kennedy children amount to anything now or ever amount to anything, it will be due more to Joe's behavior and his constant example than to any other factor. In appearance he resembled his mother and he inherited from her a singular consideration and love for younger people and the gift of winning their affections immediately. From his father, Joe inherited a tremendous drive and capacity for work and a flowing and infectious vitality. Things did not come easy to him. I think his accomplishments were due chiefly to the amazing intensity with which he applied himself to the job at hand. I do not think I can ever remember seeing him sit back in a chair and relax. Even when he was still, there was always a sense of motion forcibly restrained about him. And yet this continuous motion did not have its roots in restlessness or nervousness but rather it came from his intense enthusiasm for everything he did and from his exceptional stamina." In the opinion of people who know Jack this description of Young Joe's air of forcibly restrained motion seems also to fit Jack himself.

Young Joe's death was heroically splendid. After he received his commission as a Navy pilot, he went to England in September, 1943, and flew a strenuous tour of combat duty that winter, most of it in bad weather, with a squadron of Liberator bombers attached to the British Coastal Command on anti-submarine patrols over the Bay of Biscay, the English Channel and the North Sea. Completing the required number of missions that made him eligible for a return to stateside duty, Young Joe talked his crew into staying on with him in Europe for a second tour until after the D-Day invasion of Normandy in June.

In July, after the second tour of duty, Young Joe had received orders to go home when he heard about an intriguing experimental mission that had been assigned to the Naval bomber command in Britain. London was then being blasted by German V-2 rockets that were fired across the Channel too high and too fast to be tracked for interception on radar screens. The enemy base from which the B-2s were launched was too heavily fortified to be damaged effectively by a bombing from the air. It was decided that one of the Navy's PBY4 Liberator bombers would be loaded with 22,000 pounds of TNT explosives and taken into the air by two men, a pilot and a co-pilot, who would jump from the plane by parachute near the Channel coast after setting its flight controls and fixing the fuses of the explosives. Two escorting Vega Ventura planes would then guide the unmanned bomber by radio to the rocket base and send it into a dive on the target.

Kennedy immediately volunteered to be one of the pilots of the explosive-laden Liberator. His luggage, which had already been put on a New York-bound transport ship, had to be removed hastily at the last minute before the vessel sailed from England. His co-pilot was Lieutenant Wilford J. Wiley of Fort Worth, Texas, a regular Navy man, six years older than the twenty-nine-year-old Kennedy, and a father of three children.

The two pilots managed to get the heavily loaded bomber into the air safely and guided it to its cruising altitude. Just before they were scheduled to parachute from the plane, apparently as they were setting the fuses of the explosives, something went wrong. The plane blew up in two quick blasts and disintegrated in midair. Neither of the bodies was recovered.

When the Kennedys received the news of Young Joe's death, Jack was at the Navy hospital in Chelsea, Massachusetts, near his father's East Boston birthplace, recovering from an operation on the spinal injury that he had received in the South Pacific. The rest of the family, including Kathleen, just returned from England where she had been seeing a lot of Young Joe, was at Hyannis Port. All of them were slow in recovering from their grief. The Ambassador went on grimly about his business affairs but his friends have said that for months after Young Joe's death he spent most of each day sitting alone and listening sadly to recordings of symphony music.

While Jack was still in the hospital, awaiting a medical discharge from active Navy duty, he began to work on *As We Remember Joe*. One day when he was discussing plans for the privately published book with his sister, Eunice, they were interrupted by the twelve-year-old Teddy, who had been listening with interest. Teddy said that he wanted to write something about Joe for the book, too. "Eunice started to explain to Teddy what he should write," Jack said later. "She told him to say how wonderful and strong and calm Joe was. Teddy said to her, 'But Joe wasn't calm—one day he threw me into the ocean.' I told Teddy to go ahead and write about it in his own words and we published it just as Teddy wrote it. I think it's one of the nicest things in the book."

Teddy wrote:

I recall the day the year before we went to England. It was in the summer and I asked Joe if I could race with him. He agreed to this so we started down to the pier about five minutes before the race.

We had our sails up just as the gun went for the start. This was the first race I had ever been in. We were going along very nicely until suddenly he told me to pull in the jib. I had know Idea what he was talking about. He repeated the command again in a little louder tone, meanwhile we were slowly getting further and further away from the other boats. Joe suddenly leaped up and grabed the jib. I was a little scared but suddenly he zeized me by the pants and through me into the cold water.

I was scared to death practully. I then heard a splash and I felt his hand grab my shirt and he lifted me into the boat. We continued the race and came in second. On the way home from the pier he told me to be quiet about what happened in that afternoon. One falt Joe had was that he got very easily mad in a race as you have witnessed. But he always meant well and was a very good sailor and swimmer.

Among the other members of the Kennedy family and close friends of Joe who contributed to the book were Grandfather Fitzgerald, Kathleen, Harold Laski, Eddie and Mary Moore, George Taylor, the Negro valet in Cambridge who was one of Joe's closest friends while he was at Harvard, Alice Harrington, in whose apartment building Joe lived while attending law school, Ted Reardon and Bob Downs, his college classmates, Arthur Krock, Joseph Timilty, John J. ("Black Jack") Daly, Joe's old enemy in sailing races, and some of the friends he knew in the Navy. "Joe is one of the most vivid memories among all the students I have had," Harold Laski wrote. "He was interested in everything. And there was his astonishing capacity for enthusiasms; what he liked, he liked with all his heart. He had a profound interest in politics and he had his heart set on a political career; he ofen sat in my study and submitted with that smile that was pure magic to relentless teasing about his determination to be nothing less than President of the United States." Arthur Krock wrote with admiration of Young Joe's steadfast refusal under pressure to switch his pledged vote from Farley to Roosevelt at the 1940 Democratic convention. In the book there was a letter from Ensign James Simpson, the last person outside of Lieutenant Wiley to speak with Young Joe before he died:

> I was in the plane testing and double-checking three minutes before take-off. I shook hands with Joe and said, "So long and good luck, Joe. I only wish I were going with you." He answered, "Thanks, Jim. Don't forget you're going to make the next one with me. Say, by the way, if I don't come back, you fellows can have the rest of my eggs." We never saw him again.

In the essay that he wrote for *As We Remember Joe*, Jack said, "It is the realization that the future held the promise of great accomplishments for Joe that made his death so particularly hard for those who knew him. His worldly success was so assured and inevitable that his death seems to have cut into the natural order of things. But at the same time there is a completeness to Joe's life, and that is the completeness of perfection . . . And through it all he had a deep and abiding faith—he was never far from God—and so I cannot help but feel that on that August day, high in the summer skies, 'death to him was less a setting forth than a returning.' " Jack opened the book with a quotation from Solomon, "Honorable age is not that which standeth in length of days, nor that is measured by number of years. Having fulfilled his course in a short time, he fulfilled long years." As a closing, Jack selected Maurice Baring's lines:

> . . . . When Spring shall wake the earth,
> And quicken the scarred fields to new birth,
> Our grief shall grow. For what can Spring renew
> More fiercely for us than the need of you.

Young Joe's death came as an especially hard blow to Kathleen. That spring of 1944 in London he was the only one in the family that she had to turn to for encouragement and help in the trying time when she was deciding to go ahead with her marriage to the Marquess of Hartington in the face of disapproval, on religious grounds, from both the devoutly Catholic Kennedys and the Marquess' Church of England parents, the Duke and Duchess of Devonshire. "But never did anyone have such a pillar of strength as I had in Joe in those difficult days before my marriage," Kathleen wrote in *As We Remember Joe*. "He constantly reassured me and gave me confidence in my own decision. Moral courage he had in abundance and once he felt that a step was right for me, he never faltered, although he might be largely held responsible for my decision. In every way he was the perfect brother, doing, according to his own light, the best for his sister with the hope that in the end it would be the best for the family. How right he was!"

Kathleen had first met William John Robert Cavendish, the Marquess of Hartington, in 1938 at a garden party near London which was also attended by the Princess Elizabeth. She was then seventeen, the daughter of the new American Ambassador, and Billy Hartington, as the young lord's friends called him, was nineteen. He had been mentioned as an eligible suitor for the Crown Princess. Billy and Kick, as her brothers and sisters nick-named her, saw each other frequently during the next year but when she went back to America with her mother and sisters at the outbreak of the war it was assumed that the romance was ended.

But in 1943 Kathleen gave up her job on the *Washington Times Herald* and returned to London as a war-time American Red Cross worker, handing out coffee and doughnuts to service men at the Hans Crescent Club in Knightsbridge. It was then that she and Billy became as good as engaged. She took leave from her work at the Red Cross club and went to West Derbyshire to help Billy when he ran for the House of Commons from that constituency in February, 1944, and consoled him when he lost the election. A few months later, when Billy formally told his family of his determination to marry the Boston Irish Catholic Kennedy girl, the highly elite Cavendishes were somewhat appalled to say the least. As one London correspondent wrote about the prospective union, "One of England's oldest and loftiest family trees swayed perceptibly."

The Cavendishes had been outstanding members of the British nobility since 1366. When Henry the Eighth broke up the monasteries and established the Protestant Church of England, a large share of the Catholic lands was given to his commissioner, Sir William Cavendish. Not only had the family been unswervingly Protestant ever since, but Billy's father, the tenth Duke of Devonshire, was head of the Freemasons. Kathleen Kennedy's wealth, which might have broken down religious differences with other titled Europeans, was of no consideration to the Cavendishes. At the outbreak of World War II, they were rated one of the richest land-owning dynasties of England with some 180,000 acres, including the estates of Chatsworth House, Hardwick Hall, Bolton Abbey, Compton Place and Lismore Castle in Ireland. They also had a large town house in Carlton Gardens, London, which was later destroyed by bombs during the Blitz of 1940.

The staunchly Catholic Kennedys, especially Rose, were as dismayed by the religious difference as the Cavendishes. Nobody in her family was more troubled than Kathleen herself. An unusually devout girl, educated in Sacred Heart convent schools in Connecticut and France, her Catholicism was vital to her. She discussed her problem with the Apostolic Delegate in London and tried at length to persuade Lord Hartington to agree to allow their children to be brought up as Catholics. With such an agreement, she could have obtained a dispensation permitting her marriage to the non-Catholic lord to be performed by a Catholic priest. As the next Duke of Devonshire, Lord Hartington felt an obligation to refuse to enter such an agreement. Kathleen, in turn, refused to be married in the Church of England, as the Duke and Duchess urged. That would have meant excommunication from the Catholic Church for her. The only thing left was a civil ceremony performed by a registrar, the British equivalent of an American justice of the peace, which Kathleen agreed to reluctantly as a final, desperate resort. In the eyes of her Church, this was no marriage at all, a sinful union, but not, in itself, ground for excommunication.

"Kathleen and Billy came to a sort of a compromise about the religious upbringing of the children they might have," a close friend of Kathleen recently said. "It was to depend on how important the role of Billy's aristocratic class would be in the government of Britain after the war. If the old order did not change, if the position of the Duke of Devonshire continued as before to be of importance in the government, Billy's children would have to remain as his heirs in the Church of England. But if the war changed his standing and made his title as a Duke less important, he promised Kathleen that he would allow the children to be Catholics."

Lord Hartington's parents and his grandmothers, the Dowager Duchess of Devonshire and the stately Marchioness of Salisbury, gave their blessing to the civil ceremony. The only word from the Kennedys back in the United States was a brief message sent out to reporters the day before the wedding at the Cardinal O'Connell House of St. Elizabeth's Hospital in Boston, where Mrs. Kennedy was ill at the time. She said that she was "too sick to discuss the marriage." Rose Kennedy was not at all impressed by the possibility that some day as the Duchess of Devonshire her daughter would be first lady in waiting to the Queen of England. She only knew that Kathleen was marrying a non-Catholic outside the church.

The wedding took place early in May at the Chelsea Registry Office with Registrar Frederick Stream officiating. Kathleen wore delphinium pink suede crepe, a short mink jacket and a little hat of pink and blue ostrich feathers. Her brother, Joe, who had stood by her through her crisis, was there to give her away. The Marquess of Hartington and his best man, the Duke of Rutland, both wore their uniforms of officers in the Coldstream Guards. The reception afterwards at one of the Duke of Devonshire's country places, attended by Lady Astor and many of the American soldiers who had met Kathleen at her Red Cross club, was marked by wartime restrictions—no champagne, and plain fruit cake with no icing. Flower petals, instead of rice, were thrown at the departing couple.

The Marquess and the Marchioness were able to live together for only a little more than a month in their apartment at 4 Smith Square in the Westminster section of London. Then he went into combat in France with his Guards regiment and she went to the United States, planning to stay with her family for the duration of the war. But on September 10, three weeks after Young Joe's death, the British War Office announced that the Marquess had been killed in action while leading an infantry patrol in front of a column of advancing tanks. An officer who was with him said later, "Billy Hartington was completely calm and casual, carrying his cap and saying rather languidly to his men,

'Come on, you fellows. Buck up.' Death came to him instantly."

Kathleen hurried from Hyannis Port to New York and caught the first available plane to England to visit her husband's parents. Then she moved back into the apartment on Smith Square that she had lived in as a bride and made it her home for the remaining years of her life, becoming more of a Cavendish than a Kennedy, warmly taken in as a daughter by her husband's family, widely admired and well liked by the British aristocracy and a popular guest at their country week-end gatherings. "We thought she was the best thing America ever sent to England," a London nobleman said of her recently.

Early in May, 1948, Joe Kennedy was in Paris on his way to a vacation on the Riviera and Kathleen was planning to visit him there. A friend of hers in London, Earl Fitzwilliam, a wealthy thirty-eight-year-old peer, was about to fly to Cannes in a small chartered plane to look at a stable of race horses in Southern France in which he had a financial interest. He invited Kathleen to make the trip with him. Flying at night in rain and fog, the plane crashed into the side of a peak of the Ardeche Mountains near the small village of Privas, halfway between Lyons and Marseilles. Everybody in the plane—Kathleen, Fitzwilliam and the two members of the crew—was killed. Joe Kennedy went to Privas and identified his daughter's body when it was carried down from the mountainside in a peasant's farm cart.

Among the Boston Irish Catholics, a suspicion of religious wavering on the part of any prominent church member becomes a widespread topic of scandalized conversation. James M. Curley used to relate how he defeated John R. Murphy for the mayoralty of the city in 1921 by spreading reports that Murphy, actually a good Catholic, had been in Thompson's Spa restaurant on a Friday eating a roast beef sandwich. A group of Curley supporters in South Boston also did Murphy considerable damage by going from door to door introducing themselves as members of the Hawes Baptist Club and urging people to vote for Murphy. When Kathleen Kennedy became Lady Hartington and when she returned to England after her husband's death to live among the British peerage, there was, naturally, great speculation in Boston about her status as a Catholic. Talk on the same question arose again at the time of her death to such an extent that the *Boston Post* published a story on it. A few years previously, Rose Walsh, the *Post's* society editor, attended the gala reopening of the Greenbrier at White Sulphur Springs in West Virginia. Kathleen and her brothers and sisters were also there. Miss Walsh went to mass on Sunday with the Kennedys, noticed that Kathleen used a missal and received Holy Communion and, talking with her later, found out that she had never left the Catholic Church. Returning to Boston, Miss Walsh mentioned this to Edward J. Dunn, the *Post's* city editor. When Kathleen died, Dunn asked Miss Walsh to write a story verifying her Catholicism to put an end to the rumors he had heard to the contrary. Kathleen's grandfather, John F. Fitzgerald, then eighty-five years old, was so grateful for the publication of the story that he made his way to the *Post* city room and thanked Dunn personally for it.

A close friend of Rose Kennedy who knew Kathleen intimately says, "Those catty people in Boston who were saying that the poor girl died outside the church didn't know that when she went back to England after her husband was killed she went on a long spiritual retreat at a convent. And after the war when she was invited to upper crust weekend parties at the castles of earls and dukes, she was getting up at 6 o'clock in the morning to go to mass with the Irish servants."

8

JACK GOES TO WASHINGTON

WHEN the Kennedys are described as a dynasty, the word is not used in a loose, figurative sense. Before Young Joe's death, the family expected the reserved and studious Jack to be a writer or a teacher. But when Young Joe died, it was assumed by the other Kennedys that Jack, as the next son in line, would take his place and carry out Young Joe's lofty political ambitions. Willingness to let devotion to the memory of a dead older brother change the whole course and direction of his life seemed only natural to Jack and to his family. "Just as I went into politics because Joe died," Jack has said, "if anything happened to me tomorrow, my brother Bobby would run for my seat in the Senate. And if Bobby died, Teddy would take over for him." In carrying on for Young Joe, Jack may be less consciously also carrying on for their father, who might have been the Democratic candidate for President in 1940 if Franklin .D. Roosevelt had not decided to run for a third term.

Jack did not plunge immediately into politics as soon as he heard of Young Joe's death. He thought about it and talked about it with his father and his friends while he was still recuperating at the Chelsea naval hospital from his wartime spinal operation. In 1945, after he received his medical discharge from the Navy, he worked for a few months as a special correspondent for the International News Service, covering the Potsdam conference and other stories in Europe and the first United Nations meeting in San Francisco. His style of writing then, as in his later speeches and magazine articles and in his Pulitzer Prize-winning book, tended to be rather heavily thoughtful and perhaps too erudite for the average hasty newspaper reader. In one of his INS feature stories from Dublin on the postwar differences between Ireland and Great Britain, he wrote a quotation from Richard B. Sheridan: "A quarrel is a very pretty quarrel as it stands. We only spoil it by trying to explain it." Desk men at the wire service's office in New York probably decided while reading such copy that young Kennedy would never be another Floyd Gibbons, and Jack himself decided while working for INS that daily journalism was not for him. "I felt it was too passive," he said later. "Instead of doing things, you were writing about people who did things."

Young Joe had talked about starting his climb in politics by running for Congress from the 11th Massachusetts District where the Kennedys had their family roots. The district covered East Boston, the Ambassador's birthplace, and Boston's North End, where John F. Fitzgerald and Rose Kennedy had both been born. It also took in Cambridge, where the Kennedys had gone to Harvard, as well as the strongly Irish sections of Brighton, Somerville and Charlestown where the Kennedy family prestige was high. In 1946, when Jack definitely decided to assume Young Joe's role as the family's political standard bearer, the 11th District's seat in the House of Representatives was being vacated by the previous incumbent, the renowned James M. Curley, who had decided to leave Congress to take up once again his old position as Mayor of Boston. Curley had gone to Washington from the district in 1942, beating Thomas Eliot, the Proper Bostonian grandson of President Charles Eliot of Harvard University and, as Curley took pains to point out, the son of the Reverend Samuel Eliot of the Unitarian Arlington Street Church. At one rally in East Boston, Curley described the Unitarians as "a curious sect who seem to believe that Our Lord Jesus was a young man with whiskers who went around in His underwear." In the primary before that election, Curley's Democratic adversary was J. Ralph Granara. Speaking one night at a meeting in the North End, Curley noticed Granara sitting in the front row. "My opponent is here in the audience," Curley said. "It is now my great pleasure to introduce to you J. Ralph Granara." As Granara started to rise from his seat, Curley turned away from him and pointed to a Negro air raid warden who was standing nearby.

"The crowd went wild and so did Granara, who made an effort to haul me into equity court," Curley wrote afterwards in his autobiography.

Curley's retirement from the 11th District's congressional seat gave Jack Kennedy an exceptionally attractive and rarely found opportunity to make a political debut. The vacancy required a special primary and a special election in 1946. The district was so solidly Democratic that the election meant nothing; the big objective was to win the party's nomination in the all-important primary, which turned out to be a wide-open fight between nine candidates. They included Mike Neville of Cambridge, whom the professional politicians regarded as the likely winner, and John Cotter from Charlestown, an experienced and well-liked figure in Boston political circles. The big field was a blessing to Kennedy, however. Although his various opponents were strong in their own neighborhoods, none of them had much support in other parts of the district and there was no powerful and organized city Democratic machine behind any one of the candidates.

Kennedy's disadvantage was that he was a stranger in the district. Although his parents were born in it and both of his grandfathers had been political leaders who once controlled its votes, Jack himself had grown up in New York and, as he said later, the only person in Boston whom he really knew at the time was John F. Fitzgerald, then living in retirement at eighty-three in the Hotel Bellevue, a politicians' hangout next to the State House on Beacon Hill. When Jack filed his papers as a candidate in the primary, he used the Bellevue as his address. There was no law requiring a candidate to live in the district; the previous representative, Curley, had his home in Jamaica Plain on the other side of Boston. But Curley, a former mayor of the city and governor of the state, was well known to the voters. Kennedy had no home in Massachusetts, except for a room in his father's summer house at Hyannis Port. In fact, even today, as he serves his second term as a senator from Massachusetts, his status as a resident of the state is a subject of jokes in Boston. "If he's ever elected President, he'll be the first carpetbagger voter to get to the White House," one Boston politician says. "The least he could do, for appearances' sake, would be to buy a house here." Jack's official residence is a small and rather dingy three-room apartment at 122 Bowdoin Street, across the street from the State House on the top of Beacon Hill, where he seldom sleeps. Young Democrat friends in the state legislature from Western Massachusetts use the apartment more than Kennedy does. One of the few times when his wife, Jacqueline, has been seen at the Bowdoin Street place was the night several years ago when they were interviewed in the apartment by Edward R. Murrow on the *Person to Person* television show. Their real home is an attractive house, tastefully decorated by the art-minded Jackie, in the Georgetown section of Washington, with a pleasant back yard garden as Caroline's playground.

And in 1946 when Jack was starting to organize his first primary campaign, he was not the poised and experienced public figure that he is today. Skinny and boyish, reserved and shy with strangers, unable to talk with hard-boiled ward heelers and political hangers-on in their own rough language, he seemed out of place and pathetically self-conscious in the tough tenement neighborhoods of East Boston, Charlestown, the North End and East Cambridge where most of the votes in the district were located. Friends who worked with him that spring in preparation for the special primary in June recall that he often explained apologetically, "If Joe were alive, I wouldn't be in this. I'm only trying to fill his shoes."

Joe's shoes were difficult for somebody with Jack's quiet reserve to fill. Joe was a genial and hearty fellow who liked to smoke cigars and go to the race tracks. He could walk into a tavern in Charlestown or East Boston and feel at home buying beer for a group of truck drivers and longshoremen. Jack had none of those sociable and easy-going qualities. Visiting a slum district saloon was a great effort for him. As his father said after watching him with astonishment when he was shaking hands and asking for votes on a street corner in Maverick Square, "I never thought Jack had it in him." But Jack did have in him the deep and intense competitive drive that made him work harder at things that he found difficult. Because he lacked the ease in approaching people that comes naturally to most politicians he set out doggedly to cover more streets and to shake the hands of more voters in the district than any other candidate would have bothered to seek. "He went into alleyways and climbed the stairs of tenement houses where politicians had never been seen before," says Dave Powers who worked for Kennedy in the Charlestown area. "He didn't realize how surprised and how impressed those poor people were to find him knocking on their doors. Nobody else had ever taken the trouble to come to them."

As the primary campaign went on, there was a noticeable change in Jack's earlier apprehensive attitude toward his role as a candidate. He became less uneasy and apologetic and more excited about winning. Keenly interested in the art of politics since he had studied government under Professor Holcombe at Harvard, he now found himself fascinated by the day-to-day give and take of speculation, gossip about the moves of the rival candidates, strategy plotting, speech writing and general hurly-burly in his crowded and busy campaign headquarters at the Hotel Bellevue. Even then, as in later campaigns, Jack was surrounded with eager and zealous amateurs of his own age, politically inexperienced but willing to work hard for him from early morning until after midnight. Some of them were old friends from Harvard and Choate like Torbert Macdonald, Ted Reardon and Lemoyne Billings, or from his PT boat squadron, like Red Fay who flew to Boston from San Francisco to give Jack a hand. George Taylor, the Harvard Square valet and handyman who was devoted to Young Joe, worked for the cause in Cambridge. Other young men in Boston, just out of the wartime service and at loose ends getting adjusted to civilian life, found the Kennedy campaign work enjoyable and plunged into it. Grandfather Fitzgerald, deeply involved himself, also brought into the camp a few older and wiser professional politicians who were appalled by the strong Ivy League flavor of the Bellevue headquarters and soon strayed away from it. Jack's sister, Eunice, answered telephones. The Ambassador in Hyannis Port was following the progress of Jack's campaign much more closely than Jack probably realized at the time. As the primary day drew nearer, it was Old Joe who added to the staff, as campaign manager, Frank Morrissey who had been secretary to Maurice Tobin, the former mayor and governor, and who had a wide knowledge of practical Boston politics. Morrissey, now a judge in Boston, continued to manage Jack Kennedy's political affairs in Massachusetts until last year.

The Ambassador and his wife appeared at the grand finale of the campaign, a tea party for some two thousand women voters, who, it was said, were awe-stricken by the opportunity of meeting Irish Boston's most celebrated and wealthy couple. Against the prestige of the Kennedy name, the promotion campaign of the Kennedy staff of tireless workers and Jack's own relentless door-to-door coverage of the entire congressional district, the other eight Democratic candidates did not stand much of a chance. A stirring account of Jack's wartime survival in the South Pacific, written for *The New Yorker* by John Hersey and reprinted in the *Readers Digest*, was also circulated throughout the constituency. "People in Charlestown said to me, 'Why are you for that millionaire's son?' " Dave Powers said recently, while recalling the first Kennedy campaign. "I said to them, 'I'm not for him because he's a millionaire's son. I'm for him because he's a war hero.' And on primary day we saw to it that most of the guys working for Kennedy around the polls were wearing Eisenhower jackets." Jack won the nomination, which assured him the congressional seat, by a much bigger margin than even his most enthusiastic backers had predicted. He received 22,183 votes. The combined votes of all his eight opponents was only 32,541.

On the night of the primary victory, old Grandfather Fitzgerald climbed triumphantly up onto a table in the Kennedy campaign headquarters and sang "Sweet Adeline," the theme song of his long, embattled political career. Eleven years later, when *Time* magazine was preparing a cover story depicting Jack Kennedy as a leading presidential candidate, Bill Johnson, its Boston correspondent, went back in his research to the night of the 1946 primary to find in Honey Fitz's song a special significance. "That was the last real touch of traditional Boston Irish American politics in the career of Jack Kennedy, the most phenomenally successful Irish American politician of them all," Johnson observed. From then on, in three terms as a congressman and in two outstandingly effective campaigns for the Senate that established him as the most powerful vote-getter Massachusetts has ever seen, it seemed as if almost every move that Kennedy made was against the grain of Boston Irish politics.

"In this town," a veteran Boston ward leader said recently, "a politician is a man who comes to a police station in the middle of the night with a topcoat thrown over his pajamas and says to the desk sergeant, 'You got a drunk in here named John Sheehan. Here's a buck. See that he's put in a cab in the morning so he'll get to Commonwealth Pier in time for the longshoremen's shape-up.' Kennedy didn't do that. As far as I know, Kennedy doesn't pay for anybody's funeral and seldom goes to wakes and he never seems to get anybody a job. Now what kind of a politician is that? And yet he was re-elected in 1958 by 870,000 votes, the largest plurality of any candidate from either party in the whole history of Massachusetts. I just don't understand it."

In Boston, the scene of *The Last Hurrah*, where every office-holding politician is expected to hand out jobs, Kennedy's ability to get elected and re-elected without dispensing patronage on a grand scale is regarded as one of the mysteries of the century. Bostonians point out with awe that in recent years, while Jack was serving in the Senate, his own uncle, his mother's brother, Thomas Fitzgerald, was working as a uniformed toll gate attendant on the Mystic River Bridge. A few years ago, one of the Senator's cousins on his mother's side of the family was unable to find employment. Knowing that a plea to Cousin Jack would be useless, he asked a friend to speak to Foster Furculo, the Democratic governor of Massachusetts, about getting onto the state payroll. Although Governor Furculo and Kennedy shared the same billboards during the 1958 state campaign and speak well of each other in public, there is a distinct coolness between the two men in their private relationship. Furculo's supporters feel that Kennedy avoided backing the Governor strongly in his 1954 battle for the U.S. Senate seat of Jack's friend and colleague, Republican Leverett Saltonstall. When the friend of Jack's cousin spoke to Furculo about a state job, the Governor quickly agreed to the request. "But there's one thing I ought to mention, Foster," the friend said as he was leaving Furculo's office. "This guy happens to be Jack Kennedy's cousin."

The Governor looked up, startled, and thought it over for a moment. "Well," he said, "in spite of that we'll give him the job."

At a family conference the next day, however, it was decided that acceptance of the Furculo offer might be an embarrassment to the Kennedys, and Jack's cousin was advised to seek employment elsewhere.

Various theories on Kennedy's curious tightness with hand-outs and favors are advanced in Boston and Washington. A prominent Democrat in Congress says of him: "The thing about Kennedy that sets him apart from all other Boston Irish politicians, and, for that matter, from most politicians everywhere, is that he seldom feels obligated to anybody. That's why the older party bosses have been leery of backing him for the presidential nomination. It's not so much his Catholicism or his youth. They're simply afraid that if they backed him for President, they couldn't get much from him in return after he was in the White House." An associate of Kennedy puts it another way. He says that Jack is not troubled by the weakness of most politicians, an exaggerated sense of loyalty to friends and backers that clouds principles and leads to trouble. "Jack assumes that people work for him only because they want a fellow like him in office," the Senator's staff man says. "He gives no jobs, no favors and no promises in return. Jack can say no in such a way that you feel like a heel for asking him."

A few of Kennedy's enemies claim, of course, that he does no big favors because he is not a go-through guy, that he is looking out only for Jack Kennedy.

"Frank Gannett wanted to buy a Boston newspaper in partnership with Joe Kennedy," one such critic adds. "Joe sent back word that he never has partners. Jack's the same way, a lone operator. The only person in the world who is close to him, really, outside of his wife, is his brother, Bobby."

Even Kennedy's most ardent admirers agree that he has few real intimate confidants outside of his own family. He makes his own decisions and from the very beginning of his political career he has never been anybody's protégé. His chief adviser, James M. Landis, is an expert on legislative law; Kennedy consults him mostly on matters connected with work in Congress rather than on party politics or campaign strategy. He often turns to university professors for information and opinions on issues related to their specialized fields —J. Kenneth Galbraith and Seymour Harris on economics, Archibald Cox and George W. Taylor on labor; Max Millikan on foreign policy; Mark De Wolfe Howe and Paul Freund on civil liberties; Earl Latham on political science, and Allan Nevins and Arthur M. Schlesinger, Jr., on history. But as a Congressman and as a Senator, Kennedy has avoided seeking the advice and guidance of professional politicians with what has seemed to be almost a scrupulous obsession.

Along with his aloofness from the obligation of handing out jobs and favors, one of the things about Kennedy that has marked him as an oddity in Boston is his unpoliticianlike behavior in election campaigns. He has taken infinite precautions to present himself to the public as an unpretentious, restrained and respectful young man, far removed from the familiar image of the cigar-smoking, flamboyant machine politician. "The people these days are no longer impressed by the pol in the Homburg hat with the flowery oratory and the big limousine and the entourage of hard-boiled hangers on," he has said. Kennedy squirms uncomfortably on a campaign tour when a mayor provides him with a motorcycle police escort. He has tried, in Massachusetts, to slip into small towns alone or with a few people who do not have the appearance of big city politicians. He seeks out a local resident, the secretary of the Kennedy committee in the area, who introduces him informally to local voters, usually at a plain and homy, cookies-and-coffee type of gathering. Before Kennedy came upon the Massachusetts scene, the successful Boston Irish candidates were always impassioned, rousing and abusive speech makers. "And where were you last year, Freddy, when Al Smith ran for President?" James M. Curley roared at an opponent in a 1929 campaign oration. "You were home, with your little red slippers on, reading the *Ladies Home Journal*." Kennedy on a speaker's platform is calm, reserved, unemotionally factual and scholarly, quoting from the classics and history books with the manner of a lecturer at a graduate school political science seminar. And yet his personal appeal is so strong that his appearance stirs up excitement in the audience, and at the end of his speech, no matter how dry it may be, listeners invariably jump to their feet, applauding wildly, even though, as one observer has pointed out, they may not know exactly what it is that they are applauding.

Trying to pin down the quality in Jack Kennedy that makes him seem so different from other Irish American politicians, William V. Shannon, political columnist of the ultra-liberal *New York Post* and no great advocate of the Senator, has decided that Kennedy's career, supported as it is by family wealth and family prestige, follows more of a British upper-class parliament member's pattern than that of an American Democrat. Kennedy's return to run for office in 1946 in the Boston congressional district of his family ancestors reminds Shannon of the Oxford-educated scion of English nobility who leaves his London club life to try for the House of Commons from a remote constituency in Yorkshire where his name is well known but where he, himself, is a stranger.

"When Kennedy went to Boston fourteen years ago to begin civilian life after World War II he was almost as much a stranger to the real life of the city as any young man from Iowa or Illinois," Shannon wrote in his analysis of the Senator's career. "He won the Democratic nomination in a safe district, one of Boston's poorest and shabbiest, partly because he was a handsome, presentable young man, but mostly because his father and grandfather were locally famous. Kennedy learned the problems of his district and did a good job representing it; as he later learned the problems of the state in his Senate race in 1952 and has done well working on them. But he did not learn them the way most politicians do, by growing up with them and knowing them as part of his own experience. He briefed himself on them the way a lawyer briefs himself on the problems of a new client. There is nothing wrong in this kind of political representation. Many districts around the country would be much better represented in Congress if they elected bright young strangers instead of insisting upon home-grown hacks. But the remoteness from the inner social and political life of the Boston community partly accounts for the emotional thinness which many observers have discerned in Kennedy's career."

Whether it was due to his remoteness from the inner political life of his constituency, or to his determination to avoid identity with old-style politicians, or whether it was merely a part of his confident independence, Kennedy went to Washington as a freshman Congressman, after the special election of 1946, firmly resolved to plot his own course with no guidance from his party's leaders. At the Capitol it was soon noted with surprise that he was keeping at arm's length the influential and respected House majority leader and senior member of the Massachusetts delegation, John W. McCormack, the white-haired, schoolmasterish representative from South Boston. A crony of Harry Truman and Sam Rayburn and a member of the high council of the Democratic Party, McCormack is an elder statesman whose approval is politely sought by most new and ambitious congressmen. A prominent Boston politician recalls meeting Kennedy on the steps of the Capitol, a few days after he had taken his seat in the House, and saying to him, "Jack, if I were you, starting in down here, I'd *marry* John McCormack. I'd hang around with him in the House, eat dinner with him a couple of nights a week, listen to every thing he had to say and ask for his advice." The politician pauses at this point in his narrative, shakes his head and sighs. "You know what Jack did when I told him that?" he goes on to add. "He backed away from me in horror as if I had pointed a gun at him."

One of Kennedy's first moves as a Congressman, in fact, was to refuse McCormack's request to sign a petition for clemency for James M. Curley, then the mayor of Boston and the previous incumbent in Kennedy's own congressional seat, who was at that time serving a Federal prison sentence for fraud in connection with a pre-Pearl Harbor defense contract. Kennedy was the only Massachusetts Democrat who would not sign the petition. The plea that McCormack was making in Curley's behalf was based on James Michael's alleged poor health. Kennedy checked privately on Curley's physical condition and decided that it was not bad enough to warrant a presidential pardon. His refusal to sign the petition did not help his personal popularity in Boston, where Curley was being kept in office as mayor while doing time in the penitentiary, and neither McCormack nor Curley ever forgave him for it.

As a Congressman, Jack lived in a rented house in Georgetown with Margaret Ambrose, who had worked for the Kennedy family since his childhood, as his cook and housekeeper. She tried hard to fatten up the skinny young representative. "Margaret was always serving him steak and mashed potatoes that were swimming in melted butter, but it never seemed to add a pound to him," says a friend who often dined with Kennedy in his bachelor quarters. A Boston lawyer, Mark Dalton, (who had worked for Kennedy in his 1946 campaign), often went to Washington during his first term in the House to help him prepare speeches. Dalton remembers one day when he was sitting with Jack at a meeting of the House rules committee. Another new and young congressman arose to speak. Kennedy nudged Dalton and whispered to him, "You never heard of this guy, but he's going to be a big man down here. His name's Dick Nixon." While they were in the House, Kennedy and Nixon once traveled together to Pennsylvania to stage a debate on the Taft-Hartley labor bill, which Kennedy had opposed in Congress. Only a few people showed up to listen to them.

Probably the most notable speech that Kennedy made in his three terms in the House of Representatives was one in which he argued against an American Legion-backed veterans' pension bill and came out with an attack on the supposedly sacrosanct Legion that not many politicians would dare to utter in public. "The leadership of the American Legion has not had a constructive thought since 1918," he said, among other things. After he was elected to his third term in 1950, he was able to report that he had not bothered to spend a cent on the campaign.

As busy as he was in Washington during those six years, Kennedy also managed to spend considerable time making public appearances in Massachusetts cities and towns that were far from his congressional district; he was already lay-ing the groundwork for a run for either the governorship or the U.S. Senate in 1952. "Back there in 1948 Jack had me driving him on dark winter nights over those steep, icy roads in the Berkshires to meetings of the Eagles and the Loyal Order of the Moose in places like North Adams and Pittsfield," says John Galvin, one of Kennedy's Boston friends.

For an ambitious young politician with Kennedy's influential name, financial backing, competitive drive and tireless energy, a bid for high state office after only six years in Congress was not as illogical as it might seem. The Democrats in Massachusetts are not powerfully and closely organized in one centrally controlled machine and there is no big boss who picks a slate of candidates. "We have a fine party in Massachusetts," says Patrick J. ("Sonny") McDonough, a shrewd and entertaining student of State House politics. "The only trouble with it is that we have ten thousand leaders." Any Democrat with sufficient popular support can set up an effective organization of his own. Most of the successful Democratic candidates for state office in recent years—Curley, Paul Dever, David I. Walsh, Maurice Tobin and Foster Furculo—have been lone operators with no solid party backing. Furthermore, about one-third of the Massachusetts voters are independents with no allegiance to either party and who often split the ticket.

Kennedy began to form his own state-wide organization two years before the 1952 election. The preliminary groundwork was done mostly by Tony Coluccio, a young lawyer from Cambridge who had played junior varsity football with Jack at Harvard and had helped with his first Congressional campaign. Coluccio spent almost eighteen months visiting each of the 351 cities and towns in the state. In every community he avoided the politicians and sought out prominent and respected leading citizens, mostly young lawyers, doctors, school teachers and small business men who had never been involved in any activity more political than the local board of education or the PTA. Many of them were willing to work for Kennedy. If they weren't, they suggested other local people who were interested. When Coluccio reported his findings, the follow-up work of forming Kennedy comittees in each locality and organizing them under district and county leaders was taken over by two of Jack's most valuable and talented campaign operators, Larry O'Brien and Kenny O'Donnell. O'Brien, a young man from Springfield who was Foster Furculo's secretary in Washington when Furculo was a Congressman, is a skilled trouble shooter, the closest thing to the old-fashioned type of Irish professional politician to be found on Kennedy's permanent staff during this past year's quest for the presidential nomination. The quiet, bright O'Donnell was Bobby Kennedy's room mate at Harvard and his aide on the McClellan committee. Cynical political veterans, who take a dim view of most of the earnest young men in Kennedy's camp, regard both O'Brien and O'Donnell with respect.

The most important Democratic politician in Massachusetts in 1952 was the governor, Paul Dever, a good friend of Kennedy. Dever was the logical candidate to run for the Senate that year against Henry Cabot Lodge and, if he had chosen to do so, Kennedy would have tried for the governorship. Along with most other Democrats, Dever felt, however, that Lodge was unbeatable and he wanted no part of the Senate race. He decided to play it safe by running for re-election against the Republican gubernatorial choice, Christian Herter. Kennedy had no opposition from fellow party members when he expressed his willingness to take on Lodge; nobody else dared to do it. Even the older Democrats, like Curley, who disapproved of Kennedy, looked with favor on his candidacy. They were sure that Lodge would put an end to the young upstart's political career. Lodge was fifteen years older than Kennedy. Their respective careers were quite similar in many respects; like Kennedy, Lodge was a handsome young man with great appeal to women voters, who tried newspaper work on the *Boston Transcript* and the New York *Herald Tribune* before going into politics where his famous family name was a big asset to him. His grandfather, the first Henry Cabot Lodge, was the powerful Senator from Massachusetts who wrecked Woodrow Wilson's attempt to bring the United States into the League of Nations after World War I. The younger Lodge ran for the Senate in 1936 at the age of thirty-four, defeating Curley whose Irish Catholic vote was split by a third candidate, Thomas O'Brien, backed by the then highly influential Father Charles E. Coughlin's Union Party. Curley said afterwards that he offered O'Brien $10,000 to get out of the race but that the Republicans paid him $25,000 to stay in it. Lodge was re-elected to the Senate in 1942 and again in 1946 after he left Congress to serve as an armored force officer in Africa, Italy and the ETO. In 1952, when Kennedy opposed him, Lodge was riding high in national prestige. It was the year when Eisenhower was to knock the Democrats out of the White House and Lodge was Ike's campaign manager.

The old pros shook their heads in disbelief when Kennedy unveiled his enthusiastic and energetic statewide organization of campaign workers. They were mostly attractive young married couples from the suburban station wagon set, non-political amateurs. "I don't know where he gets them, but they're all *new*," said Mike DeLuca, a veteran minor figure in Boston politics. "Guys who have been in politics here for years don't know any of them." The big shocker was Kennedy's choice for his campaign manager. Instead of an experienced strategist familiar with Massachusetts, he picked his younger brother, Bobby, then twenty-seven and just out of the University of Virginia law school. Bobby knew very little about Boston. A very prominent local politician, paying a call to the Kennedy campaign headquarters soon after it was opened, was astounded to discover that nobody in the office, including Bobby, knew who he was. "You're asking me who I am?" the celebrity shouted. "You mean to say nobody here knows me? And you call *this* a political head-quarters?" Annoyed by the politician's abusive language, Bobby threw him out.

All of the Kennedys plunged into the campaign. Eunice, Pat and Jean toured the state, speaking to womens' clubs, showing movies of Jack's career and acting as his hostesses at a series of huge and successful tea parties where the handsome young bachelor candidate shook hands graciously with thousands of thrilled ladies. Bobby's congenial and spirited young wife, Ethel Skakel Kennedy, who had been Jean's room mate at Manhattanville College of the Sacred Heart, worked long hours and enjoyed it immensely, as did Teddy, then an undergraduate at Harvard. The brothers and sisters appeared together twice in a family television show which they called, "Coffee With The Kennedys," and attended nightly house parties staged by Jack's supporters in various parts of the State. At the peak of the campaign, John E. Powers, who was directing the Democratic ticket's drive in the Boston area, went with an unusual request to Jack's father. The Ambassador had kept himself out of the public eye during the election fight but he was active behind the scenes, watching every move on both sides and seeking advice for his son from Jim Landis in New York and Arthur Krock in Washington. Powers explained that the Kennedy and Dever cause needed an extra touch of excitement and asked if Jack's mother could be brought into the campaign to give a series of speeches at rallies in Boston. The Ambassador frowned on the proposal. "But she's a grandmother," he objected.

"She's also a Gold Star mother, the mother of a Congressman and a war hero, the beautiful wife of Ambassador Joseph P. Kennedy and the daughter of John F. Fitzgerald —which means that she's hot stuff in Boston," Powers told him. "I need her and I've got to have her."

Rose Kennedy toured the city with Powers, changing in her car from the simple wrap-around skirt and blouse that she wore at union halls and street corner meetings in tenement districts to the costly cocktail dress that she displayed with jewelry at formal hotel dinners. "Rose wowed them everywhere," Powers recalled recently. "She greeted the Italians in the North End with a few words of Italian and told them how she grew up in their neighborhood. In Dorchester, she talked about her days in Dorchester High School. She showed them the card index file she kept when her kids were little to keep track of the vaccinations and medical treatments and dental work. At a high-toned gathering of women, she'd talk for a few minutes about Jack and then she'd say, 'Now let me tell you about the new dresses I saw in Paris last month.' They loved her. No, the family prestige of the Kennedys among the Boston Irish did Jack no harm. Later on, when the campaign started to dip a little, we got Rose and her daughters to go from door to door. One of the girls would ring a door bell in West Roxbury and say, 'I'm Eunice Kennedy.' The lady of the house would say, 'Oh, yes, dear! Won't you come in?' Then she'd run into the bedroom and change into a cocktail dress even though it was only ten o'clock in the morning, and she'd get on the phone and call up four or five neighbors and say to them, 'Guess who's in *my* house? *Eunice Kennedy!*'"

The presence of the Kennedy women in the campaign and the air of refinement brought into Jack's organization by his large following of high-minded amateurs made allegiance with the Democratic candidate a sort of chic social distinction. "If you had a Kennedy sticker on your car it meant that you were mixing with the right people," Powers says.

For Jack Kennedy himself, the 1952 campaign was an exhausting ordeal. He was determined to cover the state as thoroughly as he had covered his congressional district in Boston, Somerville and Cambridge in the primary fight in 1946. He was on the move constantly for eight months, visiting the larger cities eight or nine times and each of the small towns at least once, shaking hands and talking at meetings from early morning until late at night for seven days a week. His diet consisted mostly of cheeseburgers and malteds that he grabbed hastily at roadside stands. The spinal operation that he had undergone in the Navy during the war had failed to heal properly and had caused him pain ever since. Midway through the campaign, there were many weeks when he was unable to move without crutches and he began to run a constant fever. "He hated to appear in public on his crutches," a friend who traveled with him in the campaign says. "When we came to the door of a hall where he was to make a speech, he'd hand the crutches to one of us and throw his shoulders back and march down the aisle as straight as a West Point cadet. How he did it, I'll never know."

Aside from his powerful sex appeal, which became the talk of Massachusetts, there were two important factors working in Kennedy's favor that the professional politicians had failed to foresee when they predicted that running against Lodge would lead to his downfall. Lodge was so wrapped up in managing Eisenhower's campaign for the presidency that he neglected his own job at home. And there was a strong, conservative element among the Republicans in Massachusetts which had favored Senator Robert A. Taft over Eisenhower during the Republican convention. They never forgave Lodge for leading the battle against Taft and they regarded Lodge as too liberal in his political views. Basil Brewer, pro-Taft publisher of the influential *New Bedford Standard-Times*, which covers the southeastern corner of the state, endorsed Kennedy and denounced Lodge as "a Truman socialistic New Dealer." Kennedy received 37,378 votes in New Bedford to Lodge's 15,812, while Jack's Democratic running mate, Paul Dever, was getting 26,376 votes to the Republican Christian Herter's 26,045. Massachusetts went overwhelmingly in favor of Eisenhower. Kennedy was the only Democrat to survive the Republican landslide. While Eisenhower was carrying the state by 208,000 votes, Kennedy managed rather miraculously to hold 51.5 percent of the huge vote (2,353,231) and to beat Lodge by 70,737 votes. Dever, who had avoided a contest with Lodge for the senatorship, was beaten in his presumedly assured race for re-election as governor by 14,456. If Dever had done as well in New Bedford as Kennedy did, he would have won.

On election night in Boston, when his fellow party members were falling on all sides and his own opponent was running ahead of him, Kennedy left his anxious headquarters to take a short walk through the Public Gardens with Torbert Macdonald, his Harvard room mate who had worked for him in the campaign. After a few minutes of silent thought, Jack turned to Macdonald and said, "I wonder what kind of a job Eisenhower will give Lodge."

"That shows you how confident Jack can be," Macdonald said recently while recalling the incident. "He was running behind and all the other Democrats were being slaughtered, and still he didn't have the slightest doubt that he would win."

When the smoke of the battle cleared away, there was much speculation in Boston about how much money the Kennedys had spent to send Jack to the Senate. The promotion and advertising on billboards, radio, television and in the mail had been lavish. Each one of the 262,324 people who signed the Kennedy nomination papers, for example, received a letter of thanks. Because of his wealth, Jack had difficulty raising campaign contributions. A big laugh greeted one letter of appeal which began, "Believe it or not, Jack Kennedy needs money." One prominent Democrat in Lowell was invited one day to attend a Kennedy fund raising luncheon at the Parker House in Boston. "Giving money to the Kennedys," he replied indignantly, "would be like rubbing a piece of pork on a pig's backside." It was widely assumed that Jack's election had cost the Ambassador a few millions, but people who were close to the management of the campaign feel that four or five hundred thousand dollars would be a more accurate guess. Although the Kennedy organization had twenty-one thousand workers, plus another thirty thousand who "did something," most of them were unpaid volunteers. In their official expense account, six committees supporting Kennedy reported total expenditures of $349,646. Jack was listed as spending $15,866 of his own money and his father, mother, two brothers and two of his sisters were put down for $5,000 each. Thirty-five of the Kennedys' friends were reported as donating $4,000 or more. In any case, it was apparent that money was not the deciding factor in the election; the Republican state committee broke all previous records by spending $1,050,501.

Six years later an interesting story came out of the Congressional investigation of Bernard Goldfine, which indicated that Joe Kennedy might have used a substantial chunk of money during the campaign against Lodge to buy support for Jack. The story revealed a coincidence between a sudden switch in editorial endorsement by the now defunct *Boston Post* from Lodge to Kennedy and a loan of $500,000 from Joe Kennedy to the *Post's* publisher, John Fox.

The *Post* had been, traditionally, a Democratic newspaper but under Fox's ownership it became violently conservative Republican and pro-Senator McCarthy. Early in the 1952 campaign, Fox came out for Eisenhower. He was also so strongly in favor of Lodge that he tried to persuade Wilton Vaugh, the *Post's* respected political reporter, to direct Lodge's publicity. Then, later in the campaign, came the switch. The *Post* stuck with Eisenhower, but it endorsed Kennedy and the rest of the state's Democratic ticket.

It was Fox who blew the whistle on the friendship between Goldfine and Sherman Adams in 1958, charging that it had gotten Goldfine favorable treatment from the Securities and Exchange Commission and the Federal Trade Commission. While Fox was testifying at the Goldfine hearings, a member of the investigating subcommittee, Representative Joseph P. O'Hara of Minnesota, asked him about the Kennedy loan. Fox freely admitted it but said that he had obtained the loan after, not before, he decided to endorse Jack. He explained that he made up his mind to drop his approval of Lodge only because he felt that the Republican Senator had been too soft on Communism, not because of Joe Kennedy's financial assistance. Two weeks before the election, Fox said, he had tried to reach Jack Kennedy on the telephone and, through a mix-up in connections, he found himself talking instead with Jack's father. They arranged a meeting at which Fox told the Ambassador that the *Post* was about to come out for his son. After he announced this good news, Fox went on, he and Joe Kennedy discussed the loan. It was obtained the following month and fully repaid, the publisher concluded. It was also testified at the Goldfine hearings that Fox had supported the other Democrats on the state ticket after obtaining, with the help of Paul Dever, another loan of $300,000.

Joe Kennedy's office in New York immediately issued a statement to the press confirming that a loan to Fox had been made, but denying that the loan had been "discussed or contemplated" at the time of the endorsement of Jack, as Fox said it was.

"The endorsement was made without prior knowledge of any member of the Kennedy family," the Kennedy statement said. "The loan was made after the election as a purely commercial transaction, for 60 days only, with full collateral and at full interest, and was fully repaid on time and was simply one of many commercial transactions in which this office has participated."

9

ORANGE BLOSSOMS AND A SPINAL FUSION

IN the spring of 1952, when Jack Kennedy was starting his long campaign for the Senate, Martha Bartlett, wife of Charles Bartlett, Washington correspondent for the *Chattanooga Times*, invited him to a small dinner party at her home. There he met an unusually attractive girl named Jacqueline Bouvier, then twenty-two, the daughter of a wealthy Wall Street financier, John V. Bouvier III. She had grown up in New York, France and Newport. Jack learned that she was now living in Washington with her mother, who was divorced from Bouvier and remarried to Hugh D. Auchincloss, also of the Newport summer set, and that she was completing courses for her B.A. degree at George Washington University after two years at the Sorbonne in Paris and two years at Vassar, which had seemed to her too much of a school for little girls. Jack also discovered that she had a mind of her own, that she spoke French, Italian and Spanish fluently, that she was crazy about art galleries and liked to draw and paint and that she was a student of eighteenth century European history and did considerable reading in French books concerned with that period. The young Congressman was impressed, but for the rest of that spring, summer and fall he was too involved in his race against Senator Henry Cabot Lodge to have any time for romance.

In January, 1953, when he returned to Washington as a Senator, and rather a famous one because he was one of the few Democrats to survive the Eisenhower landslide, he looked up Miss Bouvier and found that she was now working as an inquiring photographer for the *Washington Post and Times-Herald*. Seeking a job at the newspaper, she was told that there was an opening for an interviewer who could use a camera. She had quickly taken the position and then hurried to a photography instructor to learn how to snap pictures. "After Jack was in the Senate, I began to see him, and then I began to see him more often, and after a few months we became engaged," she said later. Jackie, as her friends call her, was not at all interested then in any politics later than those of eighteenth century Europe. Jack took her to visit his family at Hyannis Port, where she was staggered by the unending rounds of touch football, tennis, swimming, sailing and parlor games. "Just watching them wore me out," she says of the Kennedys. Bobby's wife, Ethel, then three years married and the mother of two children with one more on the way, had established herself as one of the fastest backfield stars in the family and a better than average pass receiver. But later Jackie broke an ankle trying to play touch football on the front lawn at Hyannis Port and she has flatly refused to have anything to do with the game ever since.

As the years went on and as the Kennedys became engaged, married, and returned to Hyannis Port with their wives and husbands and children, the crowded weekends at the family's seaside home never seemed to change. A few years ago, one of their friends, Dave Hackett, described it well when he wrote *Rules for Visiting the Kennedys:*

"Prepare yourself by reading the *Congressional Record, U.S. News and World Report, Time, Newsweek, Fortune, The Nation, How to Play Sneaky Tennis,* and the *Democratic Digest.* Memorize at least three good jokes. Anticipate that each Kennedy will ask you what you think of another Kennedy's (a) dress, (b) hairdo, (c) backhand, (d) latest public achievement. Be sure to answer, 'Terrific.' This should get you through dinner. Now for the football field. It's 'touch' but it's murder. If you don't want to play, don't come. If you do come, play, or you'll be fed in the kitchen and nobody will speak to you. Don't let the girls fool you. Even pregnant, they can make you look silly. If Harvard played touch, they'd be on the varsity. Above all, don't suggest any plays, even if you played quarterback at school. The Kennedys have the signal-calling department sewed up, and all of them have A-plus in leadership. If one of them makes a mistake, keep still. Run madly on every play, and make a lot of noise. Don't appear to be having too much fun, though. They'll accuse you of not taking the game seriously enough . . . Don't criticize the other team, either. It's bound to be full of Kennedys, too, and the Kennedys don't like that sort of thing . . . To become really popular you must show raw guts. To show raw guts, fall on your face now and then. Smash into the house once in a while going after a pass. Laugh off a twisted ankle or a big hole torn in your best suit. They like this. It shows you take the game as seriously as they do."

One summer Hackett was invited to join Bobby and Ethel, Teddy, Jean, and Red Fay and his wife, Anita, on a ten day cruise from Cape Cod to Maine. They anchored their boat, one afternoon, near Northeast Harbor and Teddy and Hackett rowed ashore in a dinghy to get supplies. As Teddy was paddling past a large and luxurious yacht, where several couples were enjoying a cocktail party, a man leaning over the rail of the costly craft called to him to row a little faster. Teddy advised him to mind his own business. "Come back here, and say that again," the man yelled.

"Teddy spun the dinghy around so fast I almost fell out of it," Hackett told Red Fay later. "The next thing I knew, Teddy was on the yacht and the man was being thrown overboard and all the women were screaming and running below to hide in the cabins. Their husbands were running with them, to see that they were safely tucked away, I guess. By this time, I'm on the yacht with Teddy. The men start to come back up to the deck to deal with us, but it's a narrow hatchway and they have to come up through it one at a time. As each guy appears, I grab him and spin him around and throw him to Teddy, and Teddy throws him overboard. In no time, all of the men—there were about eight of them—were in the water. I never saw anything like it."

At the time that Jack and Jackie became engaged in 1953, Eunice was married to Robert Sargent Shriver, Jr. by Cardinal Spellman in St. Patrick's Cathedral. "It was the Cardinal's first nuptial mass for anyone outside his own family since he took the red hat seven years before," an observing reporter for the New York *Daily News* wrote. "This shows where the Kennedys stand with the Church." Eunice is the most serious-minded of the Kennedy girls. A friend of the family recalls that in her college days she would whip out a notebook and pencil and jot down notes when a guest at the dinner table in Hyannis Port said something that interested her. She studied social science at Stanford and then took a job with the State Department at the end of the war, handling the return of American war prisoners from Germany. Later she moved into Jack's house in Washington and lived with him while she worked for the Department of Justice, arranging conferences and studies on juvenile delinquency. Sarge Shriver, the handsome son of an old Maryland family and a graduate of Yale and Yale Law School, was working at that time in real etsate management for Joe Kennedy, whose vast holdings include several big office buildings on Park Avenue in New York and the huge Merchandise Mart in Chicago. The Ambassador bought the Merchandise Mart, second in size only to the Pentagon, among the world's large buildings, from the Marshall Field interests in 1945 for an estimated twenty million dollars. Ownership shares in the Mart are now divided between the Kennedy sons and daughters and the Joseph P. Kennedy, Jr., Foundation, the family's philanthropic trust, which specializes in the support of hospitals and schools for retarded children. The Ambassador was impressed by Sarge Shriver's work and sent him to Washington to give Eunice a hand with the arrangement of her juvenile delinquency conferences. Perhaps not too much to her father's surprise, they soon became engaged.

Shriver is now the assistant manager of the Merchandise Mart, as well as President of the Board of Education in Chicago. A prominent Democrat in Illinois, he has been mentioned frequently as a possible candidate for the governorship of that state. He and Eunice now have three children.

The bride's bouquet at Eunice's wedding reception on the Starlight Roof of the Waldorf Astoria was caught by Patricia, the next daughter in line, and probably the best looking of the girls, as well as the tallest and the family's best golfer with the exception of the Ambassador himself. The following winter at Palm Beach Pat met Peter Lawford, the British-born Hollywood movie star who later became the Nick Charles of televison's *The Thin Man*. Lawford soon proposed, but Pat was determined not to be rushed into marriage. She was planning a trip around the world with a girl friend from Boston and she decided to delay a definite answer to Lawford until the journey was over. Saying goodbye to Peter in San Francisco, she warned him that she would not be seeing him again for six months. She managed to get as far as Tokyo. There she realized that going on to India, the Middle East and Europe would be unbearable. With hurried apologies to her traveling companion, Pat caught the next plane back to California where Lawford was waiting for her when she landed. They decided that they would break the news to the Ambassador right away. Joe was not overjoyed at the prospect of having a Hollywood personality as a member of his family. Pat's father is reported to have said to Lawford, "If there's anything I think I'd hate as a son-in-law, it's an actor, and if there's anything I think I'd hate worse than an actor as a son-in-law, it's an English actor." Lawford, a likeable and casual fellow, not at all in awe of the dynamic Kennedy men, was not a bit perturbed by the Ambassador.

As Lawford's wife, Pat lives in an atmosphere of regal splendor. They bought the palatial beach home of the late Louis B. Mayer, the movie tycoon, on the ocean at Santa Monica. When Mayer built the place in the depths of the depression prices in 1932 he spent $250,000 on it. A courtyard, paved with marble, and a swimming pool separate the house from the beach. In the huge living room, a movie screen and proscenium rise from the floor at the touch of a button. A projection booth with two theater-sized projection machines is hidden behind paintings in one wall. Lawford's master bedroom is solid marble. They have converted Mayer's garden greenhouse into a playhouse for their three children, Christopher, five, a daughter named Sydney, three, and a smaller daughter, who is named Victoria Francis. The Victoria comes from the date of her birth, the same day that Uncle Jack won his overwhelming re-election to the Senate in 1958, and the Francis is for the name of her parents' closest friend in Hollywood, Frank Sinatra. The Lawfords are charter members of Sinatra's exclusive social group, known as The Clan, along with Dean Martin, Judy Garland, Shirley MacLaine, Sammy Davis, Jr., and Tony Curtis. Like Sinatra, Lawford drives a sleek $8,000 Italian-bodied Dual-Ghia. Peter and Frank are business partners in the ownership of a popular Beverly Hills restaurant called Puccini's. Pat and Peter also have a profitable television film company of their own, Kenlaw Productions, which owns a one-fourth interest in the extremely valuable re-run rights to "The Thin Man's" seventy-six half-hour shows. Kennedy also owns outright the films of Lawford's previous TV series, "Dear Phoebe," and is in the process of making more television comedy films.

Pat has been preparing to play hostess to all of the Kennedys during the Democratic convention in Los Angeles. She is a close friend of Paul Ziffren, the Democratic leader of Southern California, and worked for him in behalf of Pat Brown in the 1958 election campaign as a committee organizer. A close friend of her family says, however, of the Kennedy women's appetite for politics, "Pat, Jean and Jackie don't really get a thrill out of working on Jack's campaigns. They're in there only out of a sense of duty. Eunice is more interested. But Ethel is the one who really loves politics. She gets a tremendous kick out of it."

Jean, the youngest girl in the family, and Teddy, the youngest boy, both seem to be more carefree and relaxed than the older Kennedys. Jean and her husband, Steve Smith, a bright and personable son of a large New York barge and tugboat operating family, live near Jack and Jackie in Washington. Smith has been working full time on Jack's campaign staff for the past two years, handling the endless and harrowing detail of the candidate's barnstorming tours in various parts of the country. Jean spends a lot of time with her small son, Stephen, Junior, at the Virginia country home of Bobby and Ethel, her college room mate. "The trouble with being a Kennedy is that people always mix us up," Jean says. "Women are continually asking me how it feels to be married to Peter Lawford or if it's true that my husband may run for governor in Illinois." Jack and Bobby have the same trouble. Traveling recently on a plane from Boston to Washington, Jack sat next to a lady who said to him, "Aren't you afraid that those terrible labor union racketeers will do something to your seven lovely children?" Jack said, "That's not me. That's my brother." Later as the plane was landing, the woman said to him, "I hope your brother gets to be President." "That's not my brother," Jack said. "That's me."

Teddy, a strapping and husky fellow of twenty-eight who closely resembles Young Joe in physical appearance, was married by Cardinal Spellman, in 1958, to a Bronxville girl named Joan Bennett, with so much blonde beauty that the tabloid New York *Daily News* devoted its entire front page the following morning to a close-up photograph of her and Teddy leaving the Cathedral. Since he finished law studies at the University of Virginia last year, Teddy has been working for Jack. Unlike Bobby, who likes government service but has little desire for elected office, Teddy is planning to run for Congress in Massachusetts as Jack did. He was given a baptism of political fire in the 1958 senatorial campaign in Boston when he was handed the delicate task of speaking before a private gathering of influential leaders of the local Negro community, who were disturbed by the straddling position that Jack had taken on civil rights legislation in the Senate. "Teddy handled it very well," says a politician who was present at the meeting.

Jackie and Jack were married on September 12, 1953, at St. Mary's Church in Newport by Richard Cardinal Cushing of Boston. A crowd of three thousand curious spectators filled the street outside of the packed church and the ones who managed to get close enough to the bride and groom as they were leaving noticed that the Senator's face was marked with scratches. The day before in a furious game of touch football with his brothers and sisters at Hyannis Port, he fell into a bed of rose bushes while running after a pass. The bride was given away by her stepfather, Hugh D. Auchincloss. Society reporters noted that she wore a gown of ivory silk taffeta with a tight-fitting bodice and a full skirt, and that she used her grandmother's veil, falling away from a small tiara of orange blossoms and lace. The reception took place at Hammersmith Farm, the seventy-five-acre Auchincloss estate overlooking the ocean, where the bride and groom stood for two hours in the reception line receiving eight hundred guests, including Ambassador and Mrs. Robert Murphy, Mr. and Mrs. Alfred G. Vanderbilt, the Bernard Gimbels, the Robert Youngs, the Morton Downeys, Senator and Mrs. Leverett Saltonstall and Marion Davis. The couple spent their honeymoon at Acapulco. Last year when Washington Democrats were arguing about a site for their 1960 national convention, one of them turned to Jackie at a dinner party and asked her where she thought it should be held. "Acapulco," Jackie said dead pan.

The first three years of their married life were trying ones. They bought the late Justice Robert Jackson's big and handsome three-story brick Georgian Colonial house at McLean, Virginia, in the rolling hills near the Potomac River, with the hope of having a large family. But Jack's spinal condition became progressively worse and during the 1954 session of Congress he was in constant agonizing pain. He became unable to move without crutches. Talking with visitors in his office, he sat in a hard, cushionless, straight-backed rocking chair. "There was a hole in his back that had never closed up after the operation he had during the war," a friend of his says. "You could look into it and see the metal plate that had been put into his spine." Doctors in New York suggested spinal fusion surgery. But the Kennedy family physicians at the famed Leahy Clinic in Boston, especially the late Dr. Sara Jordan, were opposed to such an operation. Not only did the Boston doctors doubt the efficacy of a fusion, an extremely risky gamble, but they were greatly concerned about Jack's ability to survive any kind of surgery; he had been suffering from an adrenal depletion, apparently brought on by the strain of the terrific physical ordeal he had gone through in the South Pacific. Adrenalin protects the body from shock and infection. An adrenal insufficiency greatly increases the possibility of infection and hemorrhage during surgery. The Senator was warned that his chances of surviving the operation were extremely limited.

But Jack became determined to go ahead with the fusion surgery despite the danger it involved. A friend remembers sitting with him on the porch at Hyannis Port in that summer of 1954 after he had listened to Doctor Jordan explain how greatly the odds would be against him on an operating table. When the doctor went away, Jack glanced at his crutches and punched them with his fist. "I'd rather die than spend the rest of my life on these things," he said.

Jack entered the Hospital for Special Surgery in New York that October. Twice after the operation was performed, Jackie and his parents were summoned hastily to his bedside because it seemed as if he were about to die. "But he fought his way out of it," the Ambassador said later. "He's always been a fighter."

In December, the Senator was taken from the hospital on a stretcher and flown to his parents' home at Palm Beach for the family's annual Christmas reunion. Still, his condition was unsatisfactory. In February he was back in the hospital again for a second operation. Recovery was a slow process. For several months, he had to lie flat on his back in bed. He was unable to work in the Senate for most of the year of 1955.

But even while he was in bed, going through painful recuperation from the operations, he was unable to do nothing. He loaded his room with books from the Library of Congress and spent five months working on his book, *Profiles in Courage.* "Jack couldn't sleep for more than an hour or so at a time because his pain was so bad," his father says, "so he'd study to get his mind off the pain. That's where the book came from." He had thought about the theme of the book—the bravery of senators who stand up against the popular sentiment of their constituents—years before while reading about how John Quincy Adams had been damned in Boston for supporting in the Senate his father's enemy, Thomas Jefferson. Kennedy had had a somewhat similar experience himself the year before when Boston newspapers accused him of "ruining New England" because he came out in favor of the St. Lawrence Seaway. "This arbitrary refusal of so many New Englanders to recognize the legitimate needs and aspirations of other sections of the country has contributed to the neglect of, and even opposition to, the needs of our own area by the representatives of other areas," he declared at the time. *Profiles in Courage* recounts stirring tales of resistance under threatening pressure from voters back home by such figures as Sam Houston, Daniel Webster, George W. Norris, Edmund G. Ross, Thomas Hart Benton, Lucius Lamar and Robert A. Taft. The chapter on Taft praises him for his courage in condemning the legal principles of the Nuremberg war criminal trials in 1946, when such an unpopular opinion virtually demolished Taft's chances of winning the next Republican presidential nomination. "I have not included in this work the stories of this nation's most famous 'insurgents'—John Randolph, Thaddeus Stevens, Robert LaFollette and all the rest—men of courage and integrity, but men whose battles were fought with the knowledge that they enjoyed the support of the voters back home," Kennedy wrote in the book. "It may take courage to battle one's President, one's party or the overwhelming sentiment of one's nation; but these do not compare, it seems to me, to the courage required of the Senator defying the angry power of the very constituents who control his future."

The book became an immediate best seller when it was published in 1956. Over the next three years, it sold almost 180,000 expensive hard-covered copies and more than a half million cheaper paper-bound editions. It still sells around 50,000 a year and it has become a favorite book review assignment of high school teachers. Inevitably, there was talk that the book was ghost-written. Drew Pearson said so on Mike Wallace's television show. The following week a vice-president of the network issued an apology for Pearson's statement. Ted Sorenson, Kennedy's research assistant and speech writer, collected most of the material for the book because the Senator, confined to bed, was unable to do his own library legwork. But anybody who has seen Kennedy's earlier writings, *Why England Slept*, and his 1945 articles for the International News Service and various magazine articles, would recognize the book as his own work. Kennedy has said himself that *Profiles in Courage*'s Pulitzer prize surprised him because he felt that the book did not have enough original historical research in it to merit such acclaim.

Discouragingly, when Jack was finally able to get up and move around he still had to use crutches. The spinal fusion operation, as the Boston doctors predicted, failed to remove all of the pain in his back. Then he tried another remedy, a series of massive injections of novocaine, and this treatment gave him real relief for the first time since the night more than twelve years before when his PT boat was cut in two by the Japanese destroyer. Early in the 1956 session of Congress, he was able to put away his crutches and has never used them since.

Among some political inside-dopesters, there are still confidential whispers about Kennedy's state of health. Last year, when Kennedy was flying one morning from Los Angeles to Sacramento to pay a call on Governor Pat Brown, one of Brown's supporters appeared at the airport to meet him pushing a wheelchair. "How's Kennedy's health these days?" the Brown man asked with a sly grin. It is said that Kennedy is afflicted with Addison's Disease, a tubercular breakdown of the vital adrenal glands. This rumor, stemming undoubtedly from Kennedy's past history of adrenal insufficiency, has been more or less demolished in the past two years, however, by the impressive physical stamina that the Senator has been displaying in his barnstorming tours around the nation. On the same day that the Pat Brown enthusiast pulled the wheelchair gag at the Sacramento airport, for example, Kennedy was on the move from six in the morning until after midnight, traveling eight hundred miles by air in a small plane, delivering three public speeches, holding two press conferences, appearing in a filmed television interview, conferring privately with several California Democrats and then hurrying late at night, after a long appearance at the Los Angeles Press Club dinner, to a family reunion with his mother and Pat and Peter Lawford at the Lawford's Santa Monica home. When he finally turned in at his hotel room, with the morning newspapers under his arm, the Senator showed so sign of unusual strain. Ted Sorenson, who had been with him most of the day, had long since collapsed in bed, exhausted.

A doctor who has no personal interest in Kennedy's case pointed out recently that the basic characteristics of Addison's Disease are fatigue and weakness. "If Kennedy were afflicted with the disease to any serious extent," the doctor said, "he wouldn't be able to get out of his own way. It's very unlikely that anybody who had it could hustle around for eighteen hours at a stretch as he does on these campaign trips." Kennedy's own doctor, who asks for ethical reasons to remain nameless, says that the Senator no longer has an adrenal depletion, shows none of the readily visible skin pigmentation and discolored mucous membrane symptoms of Addison's Disease and has an above-average resistance to infections, such as influenza, which an Addisonian would not have. "His back is entirely well," Kennedy's doctor adds. "The outstanding vigor with which he meets an incredibly demanding schedule is clear evidence of his fine physique and remarkable vitality."

And so it was that in the spring of 1956, when the Democrats were warming up for their presidential year convention, Jack Kennedy was on his feet again, ready to go, go, go.

10

CHICAGO

WHEN Estes Kefauver defeated Senator John F. Kennedy for the vice-presidential nomination at the 1956 Democratic convention in Chicago, the New York *Herald Tribune* began its story, "The famous Kennedy luck ran out today." Actually, as everybody realized later, losing the vice-presidential nomination that year was one of the luckiest things that ever happened to Kennedy.

The Senator's father, who stayed away from Chicago, spending August, as he usually does, at his home on the French Riviera, had sternly warned his son before the convention not to accept the vice-presidential nomination if it were offered to him. The Ambassador argued that Adlai Stevenson would be badly beaten by Eisenhower in the November election no matter whom he had as a running mate. If Jack were with him on the Democratic ticket, Joe said, the defeat would be blamed on Kennedy's Catholicism and the hopes of all Catholics who wanted to run for high national office in the United States would be squelched for the next twenty years. Joe's theory was correct, of course, and it was fortunate for Jack that he was not linked as a Catholic to the defeated Stevenson. But it was much more fortunate that he ignored his father's advice during the convention and plunged into the free-for-all fight for the secondary nomination against Kefauver and Hubert Humphrey. By losing to Kefauver, but showing a surprising and exciting display of enthusiastic nation-wide strength while doing so, the young Kennedy emerged from the Democratic debacle of 1956 as a bright and shining new star. Not long after the convention, somebody assured Kennedy that he would be a shoo-in for the vice-presidential nomination in 1960. "I'm not running for vice-president any more," he said. "I'm now running for president."

It was said afterwards that Kennedy might have won unhappily over Kefauver if the totalizer score board in the convention hall had not been dismantled by mistake the night

119

before the vice-presidential balloting began. If the delegates on the floor had the score board before them to show how well Jack was doing on the second ballot, he might have picked up more votes. The good luck of his defeat was more widely attributed to his backing in the Senate of the Eisenhower-Benson flexible farm price supports, which made him unpopular in the farm belt, and to his battle a few months earlier against the respected House majority leader, John W. McCormack, for control of the Massachusetts delegation to the convention. Although Kennedy's successful duel with McCormack, his first real taste of intra-party intrigue and in-fighting, was an impressive display of power, it was costly to him in Chicago. McCormack, the respected senior member of the party's high council in Washington, is admired by influential Democrats. Kennedy's cool disregard for him opened many eyes for the first time to the young Senator's unmanageable independence. As one observer remarked after Kennedy was beaten by Kefauver, "How much easier to say, 'I voted against Kennedy because of his farm vote,' than 'I voted against Kennedy because some congressional leaders resented the manner in which he supplanted Majority Leader McCormack as the spokesman for his party in Massachusetts.'"

The struggle for control of the Massachusetts delegation that spring was really more of a showdown between Kennedy and William H. ("Onions") Burke, Jr., the chairman of the state Democratic committee, than between Kennedy and McCormack himself. Burke, a McCormack henchman, wanted to send the Massachusetts delegation to Chicago pledged to the favorite son presidential candidacy of McCormack. This was not at all an unreasonable attitude because McCormack as a favorite son had won the April write-in presidential primary in Massachusetts. But Kennedy and Paul Dever wanted an unpledged delegation that could be thrown to their presidential choice, Adlai Stevenson, on the first ballot. McCormack, like his friend, Harry Truman, and other old guard Democrats, was not too keen on Stevenson at the time. Burke made the error of saying that anybody in favor of Stevenson "ought to be in Princeton listening to Alger Hiss." Kennedy does not take that sort of talk. Moving in with a skill that surprised many of the Boston politicians, he undermined Burke and replaced him with a state chairman of his own choosing, John M. Lynch, a former mayor of Somerville; and it was Kennedy, not

McCormack, who went to Chicago as head of the Massachusetts delegation.

When the convention opened, Hubert Humphrey was the only announced vice-presidential candidate. To all appearances, Kennedy was there only as the narrator of the Democratic campaign movie, *The Pursuit of Happiness*, which opened the proceedings. When National Chairman Paul Butler called him to the platform to take a bow after the film was shown, the party leaders were somewhat taken aback by the big and warm ovation that he received. There was a hurried conference backstage, and at one o'clock that morning Kennedy was asked to deliver the next day's speech of nomination for Stevenson, with only twelve hours to prepare it. The speech was not a masterpiece but it focused the attention of the convention and of the television-watching nation on Kennedy and in the spotlight he made an attractive impression. Some of his lines went over big. The delegates went wild when he said, of Eisenhower and Nixon, "One takes the high road and one takes the low road."

During the interval between the nomination of Stevenson on that second afternoon of the convention and his acceptance which he was to announce that night, friends of Kennedy began to work on getting Jack the vice-presidential nomination. Back in June, Governor Abraham Ribicoff of Connecticut, then as now a staunch admirer of Kennedy, and Governor Dennis J. Roberts of Rhode Island had plugged him for the second spot on the ticket. They had been joined by two of Jack's friends in the Senate, George Smathers of Florida and Albert Gore of Tennessee, and a Congressman from Western Massachusetts, Edward P. Boland. In Chicago, after Kennedy nominated Stevenson, Ribicoff, Roberts, Mayor Richard Daley of Chicago and Governor John S. Battle of Virginia went to see Stevenson and talked him into leaving the choice of a vice-presidential nominee up to the convention delegates instead of picking his own as the presidential candidate usually does.

That was the beginning of a long and feverishly busy night for all of the Kennedys except the Ambassador, who was in France, and Pat, who was home in California awaiting a baby. The others gathered with Jack and his lieutenants —Ted Sorenson, Ted Reardon, Larry O'Brien, Kenny O'Donnell, Torbert Macdonald, Johnny Powers—in a suite at the Conrad Hilton hotel, to decide what to do. A movement was growing among the Southerners to stop Kefauver and word came to the room that the Georgia delegation had caucused in favor of Kennedy. "By God!" Jack cried. "If Georgia will vote for me, I must have a chance. I'll go for it." Bobby rushed out to get Kennedy banners and posters printed. Everybody else scattered all over the city seeking delegates. Even Peter Lawford, back in Santa Monica with Pat, got on the telephone and located in Chicago his friend from the Desert Inn in Las Vegas, Wilbur Clark, chairman of the Nevada delegation. Clark promised to give Kennedy thirteen and a half of Nevada's fourteen votes.

When the balloting started the next day, Jack had been able to get only two hours sleep in forty-eight; he had been up all night seeking support and he had also been awake all of the night before that preparing the speech of nomination for Stevenson. He moved into a room in the Stock Yard Inn, next to the convention hall, and undressed to take a bath and to go to bed for a while. As he undressed, he watched the voting on a television screen in his room. On the first ballot, he received 304 votes to Kefauver's 483½. His friend, Gore of Tennessee, had 178 and Mayor Robert Wagner of New York had 162¼ while Humphrey trailed with 134½.

But on the second ballot Kennedy began to soar. Arkansas switched from Gore to him. New Jersey, South Carolina and Mississippi went for Kennedy. Lying on his bed in his underwear, Jack watched Lyndon Johnson arise to announce that Texas was giving its votes "to the fighting sailor who wears the scars of battle." Sarge Shriver put his head in the door to say that, in view of what was going on at the convention, Charles Potter, the manager of the Stock Yard Inn, thought it advisable to move Jack to a larger air-conditioned suite. Kennedy arose and took a quick shower. When he came out of the bathroom and started to dress, he was within 38½ votes of the nomination. Ted Sorenson, who was with him, reached for his hand to congratulate him. "Not yet," Jack said. While he was putting on his shirt, Tennessee switched from Gore to Kefauver. Then Missouri, which had been supporting Humphrey, gave its 31½ votes to Kefauver. By the time Kennedy finished dressing he was beaten. "Let's go," he said calmly to Sorenson, and hurried to the convention hall to make a speech giving Kefauver his support.

Still hotly debated among Democrats, especially among Boston Democrats, is the question of whether or not John McCormack retaliated for his loss of leadership in the Massachusetts delegation by giving Kennedy the leg on the convention floor during the excited final voting. Several spectators insist that it was McCormack, standing beside Tom Hennings, chairman of the Missouri delegates, who signaled to his friend, the convention chairman, Sam Rayburn, to recognize Hennings. When Hennings got the nod from Rayburn, he announced Missouri's switch to Kefauver and crushed Kennedy's hopes.

McCormack has vehemently denied that he was asking Rayburn to recognize Hennings. He says that he was trying to call Rayburn's attention to the Kentucky delegation, which wanted to switch to Kennedy. Kennedy himself is now unconcerned about the matter. "If McCormack wanted to put the knife into me, he had every right to do so," he said a while ago. "That's politics. Anyway, as things turned out, Missouri did me a big favor when it switched to Kefauver, although I must admit I didn't think so at the time."

The old pros in the Democratic party, who deplore Kennedy's refusal to hire experienced strategists of the Jim Farley-Ed Flynn-Bob Hannegan type, claim that the Kennedy performance in Chicago was badly managed. They pick it apart critically and hold it up as an example of how much Jack needs an older head in his corner.

"He did well, but he would have done much better if he had somebody with him who knew the score instead of all those crew-cut college boys in their silk suits," one veteran says. "I saw with my own eyes Mayor Daley of Chicago asking two of them where Jack was and they turned away from him because they didn't recognize him. He only wanted to tell Jack that Stevenson was throwing the vice-presidential thing wide open. And they kept Carmine De Sapio waiting outside Jack's hotel room for a half hour at 1:30 in the morning when he was trying to deliver ninety-two New York votes. Nobody knew it was De Sapio."

Another old-timer was standing next to James A. Farley on the convention floor when the Kennedy bandwagon was beginning to roll. "Who's going to nominate him?" Farley asked. The other man said that Kennedy's name would be placed before the convention by his staunch ally, Governor Ribicoff of Connecticut. Farley raised his eyes toward heaven in horrified disapproval. "Why don't they get somebody they haven't got?" he asked. In other words, according to Farley's fundamentals of convention strategy, if you are making a close fight you give the honor and the spotlight of a nominating speech to a prospective backer whom you have not yet captured instead of wasting such a lure on a friend whom you already have in your pocket.

When the tide was turning against Hubert Humphrey, a plum that dangled attractively before the eyes of both Kennedy and Kefauver was Humphrey's bloc of Minnesota votes. One of the Minnesota delegates was approached by a Kennedy aide during that dark hour. "Jack's in his room at the Stock Yard Inn," the Kennedy man said. "He wants Hubert to come over and see him."

The Minnesotan said later, "It was an incredible boner, and somebody should have pointed it out to Jack. He wanted Humphrey's votes, and instead of coming to Humphrey and asking for them, he was asking Humphrey to come to him. A half hour later, old Estes Kefauver came lumbering in to our meeting and sat down and said, 'Hubert, what can you do for me?' At that time, we couldn't do anything for either of them, but if we could have, which one do you think we would have helped? The guy who summoned Hubert to the Stock Yard Inn? Or the fellow who came to us, humbly and politely, with his hat in his hand, asking for a little help?"

Kennedy's staff men say that their effort in Chicago was poorly organized because Jack had no idea until the night before the balloting began that he was going to run for the nomination. "Don't you think we would have had some banners printed if he did know that he was going to run?" one of them says. However, Kennedy must have had some vice-presidential notions. The day before he went to Chicago he spent the afternoon in the New York studio of Arnold Newman, the famed photographer, having pictures of himself made. Newman remembers that not many portraits were snapped because Kennedy spent most of the time that he was in the studio answering long distance telephone calls from various parts of the country. "I also remember he was wearing socks that didn't match," Newman says.

Kennedy took his defeat hard at first, not realizing that his showing at the convention had made him an attractive figure in national politics and that he was fortunate not to have his name on the Democratic ticket in the coming election. He left Chicago in a state of exhaustion, withdrawn, tense and preoccupied. It was a miserable time for his wife. She was seven months pregnant, ill and lonely. She had stayed with Eunice and Sarge Shriver in Chicago and had seen

Jack from a distance only a few times when he had wandered past the box where she was sitting at the convention. To make it worse for her, Jack announced as they were leaving Chicago that he was flying directly to France to spend a couple of weeks' vacation with his father. Jackie went to her mother in Newport.

Four days after she arrived in Newport, Jackie was rushed to a hospital for an emergency operation and lost her baby. She became seriously ill. Jack was notified by telephone in Southern France and rushed back by plane immediately. He spent two weeks in Newport, sitting every day with Jackie in her hospital room. Then he was gone again, campaigning for Stevenson, and she saw little of him for the next two months. In one five-week period during the 1956 campaign, Kennedy covered thirty thousand miles and made one hundred and fifty speaking appearances in twenty six states. Because of the big hit he had made at the convention, he was in demand at Democratic rallies everywhere. "When you're constantly on the move like that, you never have a chance to get your laundry done," he said later. "I was always washing my last remaining shirt late at night in a hotel bathroom."

After the Stevenson defeat in the election, Jack and Jackie found that they had no desire to go back to the big house in Virginia where they had planned to bring their baby. They sold the place to Bobby and Ethel, who had just had their fifth child.

11

MRS. ROOSEVELT AND BISHOP PIKE

JACK KENNEDY emerged from the Democratic convention of 1956 as a figure with so much national appeal that party officials everywhere agreed with their national committee man who said, a year later, "If we held a convention next month, it would be Kennedy, period." In 1957, the Senator received more than 2,500 speaking invitations from all over the United States and accepted 144 of them. Democrats and Farmer-Laborites in Minnesota who had angrily cancelled his scheduled appearance at their Jefferson-Jackson Day dinner before the convention, because of his vote for the Eisenhower-Benson flexible farm supports, begged him to come to the same affair the following year and cheered him wildly. "Jack Kennedy has left panting politicians and swooning women across a large spread of the U.S.," *Time* magazine reported in a review of Kennedy's booming popularity in 1957. "At Daytona Beach, when a National Airlines attendant yelled angrily at him to hustle aboard or get left in Florida, Mayor J. Hart Lonk said pointedly: 'He doesn't have much respect for the future president of the U.S., does he?' To a Young Democrats' convention in Reno, University of Minnesota Co-Ed Geri Storm brought word from her fifty-six sorority sisters: 'Every girl told me to give Senator Kennedy all her love and to tell him they would all vote for him.' In Oklahoma City, a grey-haired woman gushed: 'I've come to see him because I think he's wonderful.' At a Washington dinner party, a tipsy woman flung herself onto Kennedy's lap, locked her arms around his neck, vowed eternal adoration. He appeared before the American Gastro-Enterological Association in Colorado Springs and the Arkansas Bar Association at Hot Springs. He spoke to the Friendly Sons of St. Patrick in Philadelphia, the American Jewish Congress in New York, and he campaigned for successful Democratic Senate Candidate William Proxmire in the Polish districts of Milwaukee."

Kennedy also came out of the 1956 convention with a

personal identity stronger than that of any younger politician except Richard Nixon. Like Joe DiMaggio and Clark Gable, he is recognized immediately and called by name in a crowded hotel lobby or airline terminal where Lyndon Johnson, Hubert Humphrey or Stuart Symington would pass unnoticed. Whether they approve of him or not, people know right away who Kennedy is when they see him. To most high school students, visiting the Capitol during a class trip to Washington, he is the only familiar figure on the Senate floor. They quickly spot his distinctive tall, slim, boyish figure and his unruly shock of reddish brown hair, the joy of political cartoonists. David P. Highley, Kennedy's barber on Capitol Hill, is often interviewed by reporters about the Senator's hair, which has been called the best-known forelock in American politics. Kennedy ask Highley to trim it straight on the side and to take a little, but not too much, off the top. He combs it with a little Wildroot but no water.

The only sour aftermath of the 1956 convention for Kennedy was Eleanor Roosevelt's later statement in a magazine article that she had not supported his vice-presidential candidacy because she felt he had shown a lack of political courage in failing to take a public stand on the late Senator Joseph R. McCarthy when McCarthy was riding high. Coming from the Queen Mother of his own party this has been a difficult charge for Kennedy to live down and it has cost him heavily in lost followers among the liberal wing of the Democratic organization. One New Yorker who was a prominent fund raiser in Manhattan for Adlai Stevenson has said that he could not get up a nickel for a Kennedy presidential campaign because of Mrs. Roosevelt's criticism of Jack. Her embarrassing question continues to haunt him at nearly all of his public appearances around the country. Late in the evening, just when it begins to seem as if he may be able to get by this time without it, a hand goes up in the back of the hall and there it is again.

Kennedy never did say anything publicly about McCarthy while the Wisconsin senator was popular. In the summer of 1954, after the Army-McCarthy hearings, when the Senate was debating on a proposed censure action against McCarthy, Kennedy wrote a speech on the question which he planned to deliver in the Senate on July 31. The speech, which can now be found in Kennedy's files, urged that grounds for the censure should be limited to a condemnation of McCarthy's abuse of senatorial privilege in allowing his assistant, Roy

Cohn, to threaten the Army in order to get preferential treatment for Cohn's and McCarthy's friend, Private David Schine. "For these reasons alone," Kennedy said in the speech concerning the Cohn-Schine issue, "I shall vote to censure the Junior Senator from Wisconsin." He said in the speech that he was opposed to a broader censure based on McCarthy's Red-hunting methods and motives.

But Kennedy's speech was never delivered in the Senate. Before he had an opportunity to put it on the record, Senator Wayne Morse pleaded that public discussion of McCarthy in the Senate in connection with debate on the censure motion was getting out of hand. Morse asked to have the matter settled behind closed doors by a special committee. The motion was passed and no more speeches on the McCarthy censure were permitted in the Senate.

It was natural that Kennedy should have disapproved of Roy Cohn. When one of the Kennedys declares war on somebody, all of the other members of the family rush to his side. Bobby Kennedy almost came to blows with Cohn one day before a national television audience during the Army-McCarthy hearings. After managing Jack's 1952 campaign for the Senate, Bobby worked for Senator McCarthy on the McCarthy senate investigations committee. It was Bobby who did the fact-finding on shippers who were sending strategic materials to Communist-controlled countries that McCarthy exposed in 1953. The younger Kennedy could not get along with Cohn, the committee's chief counsel, and he walked out of his job. But he returned in February, 1954, not to work for McCarthy and Cohn, but to serve as counsel for the Democratic minority members of the committee, which included Senator John L. McClellan, Senator Stuart Symington and Senator Henry M. Jackson. On the day that Bobby became embroiled with Cohn during the Army-McCarthy hearings, McCarthy had been cross-examined sharply by Jackson. Cohn rushed to Kennedy afterwards and warned him, Bobby said later, that he was going to "get" Jackson the next day by charging that Jackson had once written something that was pro-Communist. Cohn denied this, insisting that Kennedy was merely indulging "in a long-standing personal hatred for me," and protesting that Bobby had no right to serve as counsel for the Democrats when his dislike for Cohn was so well known. "If I have any dislike, it's well justified," Bobby snapped at him.

When Jack Kennedy was preparing to deliver his speech

on the censure of McCarthy, he was crippled by his spinal disorder. The following October when the censure motion came up for a vote in the Senate Kennedy was in the hospital in New York. He could have gone on the record for or against the censure by pairing his vote with that of another absent colleague who held an opposite view. Kennedy refrained from taking a stand on the motion. He says that the grounds for the censure had been extended far beyond the Cohn-Schine issue and that he was unable to follow from his hospital bed what was going on in the Senate because he was in pain and under sedation at the time. Since then, he explains, he has studied the censure of McCarthy and has decided that it was just and proper.

This explanation cuts no ice with Kennedy's critics in the liberal wing of his party who agree with Mrs. Roosevelt that he ducked the issue because of the strong pro-McCarthy sentiment of his Irish Catholic constituents in Massachusetts. The same people like to point out that Kennedy straddled the civil rights bill in 1956, voting on one section of it with the North and on another with the South. They have joined with the Republicans in giving widespread circulation to a now well-worn play on the title of the book, *Profiles in Courage*, the joke about the Senator being a young man who should show less profile and more courage.

Kennedy has been just as roundly chastised by conservatives for not being in favor of McCarthy. In July, 1959, after he wrote a favorable review for the Washington *Post and Times Herald* of Richard Rovere's critical biography of McCarthy, the *Chicago Tribune* in its leading editorial damned the Senator as a hypocrite. After quoting from Kennedy's review ("A cult of devotees is not the only trace of the McCarthy contagion that remains today . . . Many who were directly affected—who lost jobs or friends or status— will neither forget nor forgive. And the indirect effects—in our educational system, our foreign service, our image abroad and scores of other areas—may be with us for at least the duration of the 'cold war'."), the *Tribune* declared: "All this is eyewash but it meets the requirements of the 'liberal' gospel. It ought to satisfy even Mrs. Roosevelt, who once found it 'unforgivable' to think that Alger Hiss and Lauchlin Currie, one of her husband's White House assistants, might be Communists. Senator Jack, after due delay, has found it prudent to be nimble in his response to the demands of the orthodox 'liberal' dogma, but as a 'profile in courage' he resembles a mess of squash after it has been put through a sieve."

As a matter of fact, Kennedy at the time was too irked by Mrs. Roosevelt to appease her. A few months before, she had appeared at a hearing in Washington on a minimum wage law where Kennedy was presiding. After the hearing, other members of the committee crowded around Mrs. Roosevelt to pay her their respects. She inquired sweetly, "And where is Mr. Kennedy? I would have liked to say hello to him." Mr. Kennedy had pointedly turned his back on her and had left the room without a word. However, on January 2nd, 1960, the day that Kennedy announced his candidacy for the 1960 Democratic presidential nomination, he participated with Mrs. Roosevelt in a panel discussion on foreign policy at Brandeis University in Massachusetts and they seemed cordial to each other.

Many congressmen and senators of both parties in Washington who have no great personal liking for Kennedy say privately that in their opinion he shows more political courage than most ambitious office seekers. They point to his stubborn stand in 1954 and 1956 in favor of the Eisenhower administration's flexible farm supports, despite the warnings from his party leaders that such a vote would cost him a place on their national ticket, as it did. Later, he admitted that flexible supports were a flop. He went against his New England voters, not only on the St. Lawrence Seaway, for which some newspapers called him "The Suicide Senator," but on such issues as Eisenhower's liberalized international trade program, aid to Communist Yugoslavia and Poland, and the abolition of the loyalty oath for G.I. educational loan applicants all of which he loudly backed. An interesting example of Kennedy's readiness to buck popular opinion was his reaction to the closing of the Murphy General Hospital in Waltham, Massachusetts, a small matter of no national significance, but a big and hot controversy in Waltham. The Defense Department announced that it was shutting down the Army hospital for a good reason; its hired help outnumbered the patients, five to one. Kennedy was deluged by 1,200 protests from Waltham, and was visited in his Washington office by a large delegation of Federal employees from Massachusetts who demanded that he oppose the closing of the hospital. The hospital was bound to be closed anyway, and Kennedy could have saved face in Waltham by going through the motions of a protest. But he enraged his constituents by openly supporting the Defense Department's decision. He wrote to each one of the protesting voters: "I honestly felt upon examination of all the facts concerning Murphy General Hospital that its continuance could in no way be justified economically." At the same time, Kennedy made a speech in the Senate demanding that the United States should help Algeria get its independence from France. The State Department and France were incensed and he was roasted editorially in Europe and at home. From Waltham came an indignant telegram: "Algeria is important but so is Murphy General."

Kennedy made quite an impressive show of courage three years ago, when he appeared at a Young Democrats' dinner in Jackson, Mississippi, during the height of the Battle of Little Rock. He was strongly advised to keep out of the South at that stormy time; if he said anything friendly to his hosts, the Northern liberals would turn on him, and if he spoke in favor of desegregation he would lose the Southern support he had won at the Chicago convention. But Kennedy had accepted the invitation from Mississippi before the Little Rock crisis and he refused to squirm out of it.

When he arrived in Jackson, the newspapers there carried a challenge addressed to him by the Republican state chairman, Wirt Yeager, Jr., to state his views on segregation. At the dinner that night Kennedy found the audience staring at him expectantly. He made a few attempts at reassurance by remarking that it is always possible for Democrats to disagree with each other. The silence grew heavier. Then he mentioned Yeager's challenge and said, "I have no hesitancy in telling the Republican chairman the same thing I have said in my own city of Boston, that I accept the Supreme Court Decision as the supreme law of the land. I think most of us agree on the necessity to uphold law and order."

The chill in the room became icy. There was a long moment of silence. Then Kennedy leaned forward dramatically and said, "And now I challenge the Republican chairman to tell us where he stands on Eisenhower and Nixon!"

The crowd leaped to its feet and went wild with applause. A local congressman said later to a reporter, "I never thought I'd see anybody in Central Mississippi speak up for integration and get a standing ovation." While expressing his respect for the Supreme Court, Kennedy had neatly dumped the blame for Little Rock on the Eisenhower administration. A correspondent for *Time* magazine who was present heard one of the Young Democrats saying as he pumped Kennedy's hand, "All these Baptists and Methodists are going to vote for you, my Catholic friend, and I'm one of them."

The best example of Kennedy's willingness to stick his neck out politically is his involvement in labor law legislation. "You can't suggest any kind of a change in labor laws without getting a lot of influential people sore at you," another Democratic senator says. "Kennedy gets jumped on by Barry Goldwater and the big business people and by the White House and he also gets himself called a traitor by the labor unions when he tries to make a compromise with the Republicans. But still he has stayed in there with both feet, trying to push labor reforms. It is hardly a field of endeavor that a cute and cautious candidate would care to get into ."

For the past two years, Kennedy has tried desperately to go into the 1960 campaign as the author of a new labor law that would satisfy both his brother Bobby and George Meany—something that would curb the Jimmy Hoffa type of union dictator and at the same time be acceptable to the AFL-CIO leaders. Republicans in Washington have been as desperately anxious to keep Kennedy from getting credit for such a law, and they have been largely successful. In 1958, with the Republican senator from New York, Irving M. Ives, Kennedy sponsored the Kennedy-Ives bill which was defeated in the House. Ives said later that "one of the chief factors" in its defeat was the fact that it had Kennedy's name on it, and added that he thought the attitude of his fellow Republicans on the measure was "pretty small potatoes."

Last year Kennedy tried again with the same bill in co-sponsorship with another Democrat, Senator Sam J. Ervin of North Carolina, because he could not find a Republican willing to back him. Bobby's boss on the Senate Rackets Committee, Senator McClellan, went along with the Kennedy-Ives bill, but McClellan wanted a law tougher on labor than the Kennedy-Ervin bill. Compromising here and there with the Republicans and Southern Democrats, Kennedy engineered his bill through the Senate successfully. But when it came before the House, President Eisenhower attacked it hard on a national television appearance, urging the stiffer Landrum-Griffin bill, with its provisions on "no man's land," "hot cargoes" or secondary boycotts, and organizational picketing, in its stead. The efforts to work out a compromise between the Senate's bill and the Landrum-Griffin bill, which passed in the House, 303 to 125, were tense and bitter. With his labor adviser from Harvard Law School, Archibald Cox, at his elbow, Kennedy had a hard time in the conference room with the Republicans and the Southern Democrats, Representatives Phil Landrum of Georgia and Graham Barden of North Carolina. During one wrangle on secondary boycotts, Cox ventured the opinion that some of the legal measures being proposed by Barden might "put the Puerto Rican girls in New York back in the sweat shops." Barden said to Kennedy in his Southern drawl, "I'm tired of watching us sit here and come close to agreement and then have these intellectual outsiders nitpicking and scratching for little holes throw a monkey wrench into everything." Kennedy said, "And I'm tired of sitting here defending Mr. Cox from your attacks." In the end, the 1959 labor law was not at all what Kennedy had wanted. He tried to be cheerful about it, and called it the best bill that could be obtained, but labor was skeptical.

In 1958, Kennedy impressed the Democrats mightily with his performance as a popular vote-getter par excellence in his run for re-election to the Senate in Massachusetts. The registered vote was a record high for a year that had no presidential race, 2,556,300, and the number of persons who showed up at the polling places, 1,952,855, or 76.4 percent of those registered, was also unprecedented in an off-year. No less than 73.6 percent of them, or 1,362,926, voted for Jack. The Republicans in Massachusetts had difficulty trying to persuade somebody to run against Kennedy. Their first choice was Charles Gibbons. When George Fingold, the G.O.P. candidate for governor, died suddenly as the campaign was getting underway, Gibbons hastily backed away from Kennedy and ran in Fingold's place on the ticket. "It does not become me to be a sacrificial goat," Gibbons explained. The task of opposing Kennedy then fell upon Vincent J. Celeste, an East Boston Italian-American who took a whimsical view of his assignment. He remarked that he was running on five gallons of gas. The arch Republican *Boston Herald*, and its afternoon sister, the *Boston Traveler*, backed Kennedy and scarcely mentioned Celeste's name during the campaign, having no desire to be linked with a sure loser. Celeste got 488,318 votes, giving Kennedy a plurality of 874,608, an all-time record for the state. Foster Furculo defeated Gibbons for the governorship by 248,557 votes.

Kennedy's 1958 campaign was quite different from the one in 1952 in many respects. Jack spent only one month, instead of eight months, touring the state. But even in that limited time he visited nearly every town. The same statewide organization that had been organized in 1952 swung back into action under the direction of Larry O'Brien and Kenny O'Donnell. The Kennedys, with the exception of Pat, who was having another baby in California, came back to Boston again, although Bobby was able to spare only two weeks off from his investigations of the Teamsters' Union and was thus unable to resume his job as campaign manager. Steve Smith, Jean's husband, ran the Kennedy office in Boston. Jackie had her first taste of an election campaign; she was at the Senator's side during most of his statewide tour. An acquaintance of the Kennedys saw their car parked outside a convent in Lowell just before the election. "Jack was inside, shaking hands with the Mother Superior, and all the nuns were out on the sidewalk, waiting excitedly to get a peek at him when he came out," the observer reported to his friends in Boston later. "Sitting alone in the back seat of the car, tired and bored, grimly flipping the pages of a magazine, there was Jackie." Jack says that Jackie has become more interested in politics during the past year since the stake has become larger, but the physical work of a campaign tour is still too much for her. "When we come home from one of those trips," Jack says, "she has to spend a day in bed."

There were no big tea parties for the lady voters in 1958 as there had been in Jack's bachelor days in 1952, but the tone of the campaign two years ago reached a new high in gentility. There were many showings of films on TV stressing the Kennedys' family life and pointing out to the Republicans how nicely Jack worked in Washington with his fellow senator from Massachusetts, the Proper Bostonian Republican Leverett Saltonstall, who once confided to John Gunther that the two things in his life that mattered most to him, really, were "Harvard and my family." Such polite treatment from a Democratic Irish Catholic must have reminded the thin-faced, sharp-nosed Saltonstall that things had certainly changed in Massachusetts since the old days when James M. Curley used to refer to him as "Pinocchio." To bring the refinement of Kennedy's campaign technique down into narrow focus, there is the example of the approach he used in the small town of Weston, Massachusetts, a rock-ribbed Republican stronghold since Revolutionary times. Kennedy's main medium of propaganda was a tabloid newspaper-style brochure with many illustrations, explaining his qualifications and past political accomplishments. His organization delivered 1,240,000 copies of the tabloid to dwelling units in 351 communities. In Weston, the Kennedy papers were handed out at each door by a group of pretty girl undergraduates from nearby Regis College. The town went Democratic and for Kennedy for the first time since it was founded.

Kennedy, as Roscoe Drummond pointed out in the New York *Herald Tribune*, was the biggest beneficiary of the Democratic sweep of the 1958 off-year state and congressional elections. "First, he not only outran his opponent mercilessly but outran political history as well," Drummond wrote. "His plurality is unmatched by any Massachusetts candidate in either party at any time. The second development which encourages the supporters of Mr. Kennedy's Presidential ambitions is that other Roman Catholics fared exceedingly well at the hands of the voters . . . The event to which the Kennedy people attach the most value is the victory of Senator-elect Eugene McCarthy over Edward Thye in Minnesota—a Catholic defeating a Lutheran in a Protestant state."

Kennedy's name, in fact, has become so magical on the ballot in Massachusetts that another man named John F. Kennedy, who was a stock room foreman at the Gillette safety razor factory at South Boston with an evening high school education, has twice been elected as state treasurer simply by putting his name on the ballot, as the Massachusetts law permits, without consulting any party or bothering to seek a nomination. His position as state treasurer pays him $13,000 and allows him the use of a chauffeured automobile. John Kennedy does no campaigning; he listed his total expenses after the voters swept him into office a second time in 1958 as $100, and it is said that most of this was spent on a victory celebration on election night. This other Kennedy, like the Senator, comes from a closely-knit family. He appointed his brother, James, a naval shipyard laborer, to a $3,780 special state police sergeantcy in the treasurer's office, and made his brother-in-law, Joseph Williams, a waiter, into a senior statistical clerk at $3,000 a year. When the treasurer sought to raise his brother from the state police payroll and appoint him third deputy state treasurer at $5,820 a year, the governor's council balked at approving the appointment, suspecting that James was not qualified for the post. Treasurer Kennedy challenged the members of the council to compete against his brother in an I.Q. test. One of the councilors, George Wells, accepted the dare. The test was held at Boston University and Brother James defeated Councilor Wells, 99 points to 98 points.

State Treasurer Kennedy's younger namesake in the U.S. Senate rated highly in the national public opinion polls until the closing months of 1959 when there was a noticeable lull in his momentum, partly because of the successful Republican fight against his labor bill and because of Nixon's rise in public esteem after his verbal clash with Nikita Khrushchev in the kitchen at the Moscow fair. It was also felt that Khrushchev's appearance in the United States did Kennedy no good; many people wondered how the youthful Senator could cope, as President, at a summit conference table with a tough and cagey elder statesman like the Russian dictator. Kennedy's young looks are a big barrier in his path to the White House. Close up, he appears to be forty-three years old, but seen from a distance on the stage of an auditorium, his slim, boyish figure and his collegiate haircut make him seem like a lad of twenty-eight. An often-heard remark about Kennedy, credited to a New York political strategist, is: "He'll never make it with that haircut." Another politician in the Midwest had said that Kennedy's youthful appearance is a bigger problem for him than his religion. "It makes no difference how mature Kennedy may be," this man says, "if the bosses and the voters decide that he *looks* immature."

Much to Kennedy's annoyance, questions about his Catholicism, like the questions about his stand on Senator McCarthy, keep coming up wherever he goes. The Senator feels that he said all that there was to be said on the subject in an interview with Fletcher Knebel that appeared in the March 3, 1959, issue of *Look* magazine. Kennedy was referring to the *Look* interview when he said ten months later in reply to a question about the religious issue while he was announcing his candidacy: "I would think there is really only one issue involved in the whole question of a candidate's religion. That is, does a candidate believe in the Constitution, does he believe in the First Amendment, does he believe in the separation of church and state. When the candidate gives his views on that question, and I think I have given my views fully, I think the subject is exhausted."

The *Look* article had said: "Senator Kennedy realizes that if . . . he becomes an announced candidate he must state clearly his views on the church-state issue. Kennedy notes that he has opposed a number of positions taken by Catholic organizations and members of the hierarchy. He attended non-Catholic schools, from the elementary grades to Harvard. In Congress, Kennedy favored aid to Yugoslavia, aid to Communist satellite states and the naming of Dr. James B. Conant as our first ambassador to West Germany. Some Catholic groups opposed the first two, and Catholics generally bridled at Conant because of his opposition to parochial schools as perpetuating a dual educational system he believed unhealthy for America.

"What would Kennedy say in an attempt to quell fears that Catholicism and the presidency don't mix? In a capsule, his theme is that religion is personal, politics are public and the twain need never meet and conflict.

" 'Whatever one's religion in his private life may be,' he says, 'for the officeholder, nothing takes precedence over his oath to uphold the Constitution and all its parts—including the First Amendment and the strict separation of church and state. Without reference to the presidency,' he adds, 'I believe as a senator that the separation of church and state is fundamental to our American concept and heritage and should remain so.

" 'I am flatly opposed to the appointment of an ambassador to the Vatican. Whatever advantages it might have in Rome— and I'm not convinced of these—they would be more than offset by the divisive effect at home.

" 'The First Amendment to the Constitution is an infinitely wise one. There can be no question of Federal funds being used for support of parochial or private schools. It's unconstitutional under the First Amendment as interpreted by the Supreme Court. I'm opposed to the Federal Government's extending support to sustain any church or its schools. As for such fringe matters as buses, lunches and other services, the issue is primarily social and economic and not religious. Each case must be judged on its merits within the law as interpreted by the courts.' "

When the interview with Kennedy appeared in *Look*, both the Senator and the magazine were severely criticized in the Catholic press; Kennedy was hit, not so much for his views, as for submitting to the interview, and *Look* was rapped for questioning Kennedy because he is a Catholic. *America*, the Jesuit weekly, claimed that such an examination was directed only at Catholic candidates, and, therefore, that it was discriminatory. The Jesuit editors flatly disagreed

Look's statement that it is necessary for a Catholic candidate to give his views on matters concerning the separation of
church and state. "The interrogation of Senator Kennedy was
in the long tradition of anti-Catholic bigotry," *America* added
in a follow-up comment in a later issue. "In the background
lay the doubt: can one be a true Catholic and a true American
at the same time?"

The *Look* article probably provoked more discussion and
debate among Catholics than among people of other religions
or of no religion. Many members of Kennedy's church see
no reason why he should not be questioned on whether his
decisions as a President would be influenced by the doctrines
of the Catholic hierarchy and several of them wrote to
America to protest against the Jesuit publication's attitude.
Vincent A. Carrafiello of Fairfield, Connecticut, said in one
letter: "When *Look* stated that 'a Catholic would have to
give his views on his religion' it did not refer to a question
of theology . . . but to a political question—where does a
Catholic owe his temporal allegiance? That question has long
vexed many honest American citizens, and asking it does not
make 'bigots' of them." Robert Millett of Middlesboro,
Kentucky, wrote that the *Look* interview of Kennedy was
"the kind of illumination every Catholic candidate owes to his
fellow citizens who are worried about the nature of the
Catholic religion."

The interview with Kennedy recalled that Al Smith had
made a similar expression of his views on the separation of
the church and state for the *Atlantic Monthly* while running
for President in 1927. This brought out comparisons in many
columns between Kennedy and Smith, most of them taken
from Oscar Handlin's 1958 biography of Smith. It was agreed
that there were not many similarities in the two candidates
except their religion and their ambition for the presidency.
Smith was a boy from the city slums who wore a brown
derby, who smoked cigars and talked out of the corner of
his mouth in an East Side New York accent. Despite his
magnetic qualities as a leader, he seemed to people in Ohio a
caricature of an Eastern big city political boss. And, although
Smith was undoubtedly a victim of religious prejudice, a
Methodist running for president on the Democratic ticket in
that highly prosperous year of 1928 might not have beaten
the Republicans. Kennedy, on the other hand, is a millionaire's son, a Harvard man and an intellectual who does not

look like a politician and who has proved, in Massachusetts, that he can attract many Republican voters.

Kennedy had agreed to be questioned on his religious views by *Look* in the hope that the publication of them at that early stage of his campaign would get them aired and discussed and over with once and for all, so that he would not be bothered too much by the religious issue in printed comments about him in the months to come. It worked out that way for more than six peaceful months; there was plenty of private speculation about Kennedy's Catholicism and questions from the audience on it at his widespread appearances but there was no mention of it on the front pages. The lull was too pleasant to last. In July a study group headed by William H. Draper, Jr., recommended that President Eisenhower should let the United States assist foreign countries, if requested, with their problem of rapid population growth. In September, a study done by Stanford University for the Senate Foreign Relations Committee suggested large-scale tests of birth control devices abroad. In October, the Protestant World Council of Churches warned of a world-wide population explosion unless there was more use of natural and artificial birth control methods. And then in November, the Catholic bishops of America, meeting in Washington, announced that they were opposed to the use of public funds for birth control here or in foreign lands. Later that same day, Bishop James A. Pike of the Protestant Episcopal diocese of California asked if the statement of the Catholic bishops' policy on government-sponsored birth control would be "binding on Roman Catholic candidates for public office."

Bishop Pike denied that he was opposed to having a Catholic as President. He said that he only wanted to know if the opposition of the Catholic bishops to the United States government offering birth control information and devices "to those people who desire it" would affect the decisions, on such a question, of Catholics in high public office. But everybody seemed to agree with the New York *Herald Tribune's* comment on the controversy: "Underlying the debate over birth control is the oft-argued political question of whether a Catholic can, or should be, elected President of the United States."

The bishop's question placed Kennedy in an awkward spot. As a Catholic, he could hardly disagree with the hierarchy of his church on such a basic issue as birth control. He said thing that he could say—that he would be opposed e use of government funds for spreading birth control road, adding that he would not, however, be in favor of withholding American aid from a foreign country because it advocated birth control. But this seemed to most non-Catholics as if Kennedy was obediently following the dictates of his church on a matter of government policy. A few days later President Eisenhower helped him somewhat by declaring that the dissemination of birth control information should not be a government function. Still, the old question of whether or not a Catholic President could be free from the influence of his church had been raked up again and was burning brightly. A great many people were thinking about it and talking about it and entertaining grave doubts. The inside word from Washington was that Kennedy had been written off as a hopeless candidate. One columnist said he had heard that "the ministers in North Carolina and Tennessee were going from door to door."

But Kennedy bounced back. Early in January, just after he announced his candidacy with a firm declaration that he would not settle for the vice-presidential nomination, the big news broke about Governor Michael DiSalle promising to give Kennedy the important support of Ohio and its sixty-four votes. The experts in Washington, James Reston said in the *New York Times*, were now deeply impressed and the same critics who had said before Christmas that Bishop Pike's embarrassing question had finished Kennedy, were now agreeing that, after all, Jack was perhaps the only Democratic candidate with enough real popular appeal to give Nixon a race. "Any doubts about the seriousness of Jack Kennedy's Presidential thoughts, the proportions of his backing or the momentum of his campaign were dramatically erased by events of the past few days," the Republican New York *Herald Tribune* said editorially after DiSalle endorsed Kennedy. "The Kennedy forces have not been idle. Nor have they been bashful about letting shrewd and practical politicians like Mr. DiSalle know that Ohio's delegates cannot be stashed away in the Governor's favorite-son pocket without a fight from the man from Massachusetts. Mr. DiSalle is not one to misjudge political strength, and in this instance he acted speedily and in hard-headed accordance with his appraisal of wind directions and velocities . . . Senator Kennedy must be credited with getting off to the sort of high-geared start that is the envy of all convention-hardened professionals."

After he secured Governor DiSalle's vital support in Ohio, Kennedy plunged ahead boldly by entering the presidential primaries in Wisconsin, Nebraska and Indiana. Whatever else can be said about his candidacy, there is nothing cautious or coy about it. Wisconsin, supposedly sympathetic to his midwestern opponent, Hubert Humphrey, was risky ground that Jack had been advised to avoid. Indiana was once a stronghold of the Ku Klux Klan. By exposing himself to tests of popular strength in such alien corn states, as well as in the safer primaries of New England and in the open free-for-all of Oregon, Kennedy is sticking to the same old formula that has worked so well for him up to now in his political career—he is depending on the voters rather than on the favors of party forces.

Such are the downs and ups of politics. The Bishop Pike incident was a black hour for Kennedy but in no time he was again treating the religious issue as lightly as he did a year ago at a dinner in Los Angeles when a humorist in the audience asked him, if, in his opinion, a Protestant could be elected President of the United States. Kennedy came back with a quick answer: "If he is willing to answer questions on his views concerning the separation of the church and state, I see no reason why we should discriminate against him." The audience howled with laughter.

At such off-the-cuff ad libbing, Kennedy shines. His prepared speeches are rather heavy and unexciting, studded with quotations and historical anecdotes. Last year, at the University of Wisconsin, he quoted in the course of one rather brief speech: Goethe, William Faulkner, Artemus Ward, Woodrow Wilson, Finley Peter Dunne, Swift, Emerson, Lord Asquith, Tennyson and Queen Victoria. But when he talks extemporaneously in a question-and-answer session, he can take any subject—aid to India, Jimmy Hoffa, Soviet missiles, housing, the balancing of the budget—and expound on it at length with a grasp of facts and figures that overpowers the audience. "I believe in anything he believes in!" a reporter heard a woman spectator gasp after she listened to Kennedy ad lib passionately on Algeria and labor problems. Red Fay says that the officers in Kennedy's PT boat squadron used to gather in his quarters and get him talking on world affairs, politics and the war. "We enjoyed it more than playing poker," Fay says.

ear Kennedy was a speaker at the annual $100-a-plate at the Waldorf Astoria to raise hospital funds in emory of Al Smith. He followed Mayor Wagner and Governor Nelson Rockefeller, whose speech was long and dull. Kennedy arose and saw that the audience was bored and tired. He put aside his prepared address and looked the people in the eye. "I think it well that we recall at this annual dinner what happened to a great governor when he became a Presidential nominee," Kennedy said. "Despite his successful record as a governor, despite his plain-spoken voice, the campaign was a debacle. His views were distorted. He carried fewer states than any candidate in his party's history. He lost states which had been solid for his party for half a century or more." The listeners nodded sleepily. It was the Al Smith Memorial Dinner and everybody at the head table had been talking about Smith. "To top it off," Kennedy went on, "he lost his own state which he had served so well as a governor. You all know his name and his religion—Alfred M. Landon, Protestant."

The crowd sat up straight, astonished.

"While the memory of this election still burns deeply in our minds," Kennedy added, "I, for one, am not prepared to say to Governor Rockefeller that the Republicans should not nominate a Protestant in 1960."

The audience collapsed with laughter and from then on applauded and laughed at nearly everything Kennedy said. George E. Sokolsky wrote of it in his newspaper column: "Here was an old campaigner who understood his audience, realized that it was a tired, weary audience, gave a grand show and said many things that will be remembered and repeated. What Kennedy did was impressive. He displayed quickness of wit, self-assurance in a difficult situation, a sharp mind with keen and good humor. It was a smart performance."

In the first week of 1960, a few days after Kennedy announced his candidacy to nobody's surprise, the official headquarters of the Kennedy for President organization opened its doors in the Esso Building in Washington, a few blocks from the Capitol. It occupied seven rooms, but it was soon to be expanded to ten rooms. In one of the offices, a salesman was displaying to a group of Kennedy aides a sample collection of campaign gimmicks—a plastic hat that looks like a straw boater with "Kennedy for President" on its red, white and blue band; a sponge that swells up when thrown into water, forming the words, "Kennedy for President"; a cigarette lighter in the shape of a World War II PT boat with "Kennedy for President" on it; a jig saw puzzle that forms a scene showing an American flag, a PT boat, and the slogan, "Kennedy for President," and a cardboard cane that unfurls a banner saying, "Kennedy for President." Established in the office were the same young men who worked for Jack against Henry Cabot Lodge—his brother, Teddy, Larry O'Brien and Kenny O'Donnell. Once again, as in the memorable battle of 1952, the campaign manager was Bobby Kennedy. "If I need somebody older," Jack said with a smile a few months ago, "there's no need to go outside of the family. I can always get my father." The Ambassador continues to stay in the background but he keeps in close touch with what Jack is doing and calls up often to offer advice. A while ago he had a suggestion for a television show. One of Kennedy's aides said to him, "Mr. Kennedy, that may seem like a good idea to you, but maybe it wouldn't appeal to the average person." The multimillionaire was indignant. "What do you mean?" he demanded. "I happen to be the most average guy in this whole damned outfit."

A politician in Chicago was discussing the remarkable Kennedy family recently and shaking his head in wonder.

"When Jack gets to the White House," he said, "he'll make Bobby the attorney general. Teddy will run for Congress in Massachusettes and Sarge Shriver will probably become the governor of Illinois. The big question is, what are they going to do with Peter Lawford?"

Editor's note: On Wednesday evening, July 13, 1960, John Fitzgerald Kennedy was nominated by the Democratic Convention in Los Angeles as Democratic candidate for the Presidency of the United States. On Thursday, July 14, Senator Lyndon Baines Johnson was selected by Senator Kennedy as his Vice-Presidential running mate, a choice then unanimously approved by the Convention.

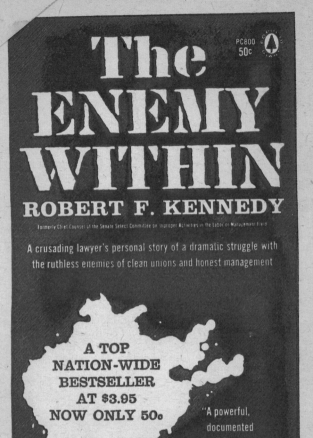

PC800
50c

The ENEMY WITHIN

ROBERT F. KENNEDY

Formerly Chief Counsel of the Senate Select Committee on Improper Activities in the Labor or Management Field

A crusading lawyer's personal story of a dramatic struggle with the ruthless enemies of clean unions and honest management

A TOP
NATION-WIDE
BESTSELLER
AT $3.95
NOW ONLY 50¢

"A powerful, documented indictment"
New York Herald Tribune

"Exciting, valuable and honest."   **New York Times**

"The findings are overwhelming, frightening, stunning in impact."   **Pittsburgh Press**

A POPULAR LIBRARY SPECIAL — 50¢

Available wherever pocket-sized books are sold.